WRITERS AND THEIR WORK

Isobel Armstrong
General Editor

Bryan Loughrey
Advisory Editor

CAROLINE DRAMA

CAROLINE DRAMA
The Plays of Massinger,
Ford, Shirley and Brome

JULIE SANDERS

Northcote House
in association with the
British Council

© Copyright 1999 by Julie Sanders

First published in 1999 by Northcote House Publishers Ltd, Plymbridge House, Estover Road, Plymouth PL6 7PY, United Kingdom.
Tel: +44 (01752) 202368 Fax: +44 (01752) 202330.

British Library Cataloguing-in-Publication Data
A catalogue record for this book is available from the British Library

ISBN 0 7463 0877 9

Typeset by PDQ Typesetting, Newcastle-under-Lyme
Printed and bound by CPI Group (UK) Ltd, Croydon, CR0 4YY

For Kay Sanders

Contents

Acknowledgements

Anyone working on Caroline drama owes a special debt to the work and example of Martin Butler, and I am happy to acknowledge my massive personal debt here. I only hope my arguments (though they may not always be ones he would necessarily share) are a credit to his influence.

Other people have been of special help and assistance in the formation and, indeed, completion of this project. Many thanks to Isobel Armstrong for her initial encouragement for, and continued engagement with, the subject, and to Ed Larrissy, Kate Chedgzoy, and Sue Wiseman for invaluable advice along the way. David Amigoni first alerted me to Edmund Gosse's account of the 'grotesque riot' of language that constituted Caroline drama. My thanks too to all those colleagues at conferences and seminars who, in their generous offers of ideas and advice, have contributed to this project. Special thanks to Hero Chalmers for our continuing and endlessly fruitful dialogue on gender and performance in the early modern period. John Higham has, as ever, been of immeasurable practical and personal help.

The dedication acknowledges the person who first shaped my love of theatre, and who continues to be my avid theatregoing companion and the very best of friends, my mother Kay.

Biographical and Historical Outline

Philip Massinger   *born* 1583   *died* 1640
John Ford   *born* 1586   *died c.*1640
James Shirley   *born* 1596   *died* 1666
Richard Brome   *born c.*1590   *died c.*1653

THE REIGN OF CHARLES I: 1625–49

1625   Death of James I; accession of Charles I; marriage of Charles
        I to Henrietta Maria of France
        Massinger becomes chief dramatist of Blackfriars Theatre
        after death of John Fletcher; Lady Elizabeth's Men at
        Cockpit Theatre become Queen Henrietta's Men
        Philip Massinger's *A New Way to Pay Old Debts*
1626   Forced Loan controversy
        Henrietta Maria performs in Racine pastoral at court
        Philip Massinger's *The Roman Actor*
        Ben Jonson's *The Staple of News*
1627   Death of Thomas Middleton
1628   Petition of Right submitted to Parliament; Duke of
        Buckingham assassinated
        Richard Brome's *The Northern Lass*
        John Ford's *The Lover's Melancholy*
1629   Dissolution of Parliament: beginning of period of Personal
        Rule (1629–40)
        Salisbury Court Theatre built; French acting troupe
        including women actors perform at the Blackfriars Theatre
        and at court
        John Ford's *The Broken Heart*
        Ben Jonson's *The New Inn*

1630   John Ford's *'Tis Pity She's a Whore*
1631   Death of John Donne
       James Shirley's *The Traitor*
1632   Philip Massinger's *The City Madam*
       Ben Jonson's *The Magnetic Lady*
       James Shirley's *The Ball*
       Richard Brome's *The Weeding of Covent Garden*
1633   William Laud becomes Archbishop of Canterbury
       Henrietta Maria commissions and rehearses Walter Mon-
       tagu's *The Shepherd's Paradise*; William Prynne publishes
       Histriomastix in part attacking the queen's court theatricals;
       is arrested and tortured
       John Donne's poems published
       Death of George Herbert; publication of *The Temple*
       James Shirley's *A Bird in a Cage*
       Ben Jonson's *A Tale of a Tub*
1634   John Milton's *A Mask Presented at Ludlow Castle* also known
       as *Comus*
1635   Richard Brome's *The Sparagus Garden*
1636   Richard Brome's *The Queen and Concubine*
1637   Resistance to Ship Money payments; death of Ben Jonson;
       theatres closed due to plague epidemic; James Shirley
       travels to Dublin; directs production of *The Alchemist*
       John Milton's 'Lycidas'
       Richard Brome's *The English Moor*
1638   Richard Brome's *The Antipodes*
1639   First Bishop's War
       No more heard of John Ford after this date
       Richard Brome's *A Mad Couple Well Matched*
1640   Second Bishop's War; Short Parliament; Long Parliament
       summoned; Impeachment of Archbishop Laud
       Death of Massinger; James Shirley returns from Ireland to
       become chief dramatist for Blackfriars Theatre
       Richard Brome's *The Court Beggar*
       James Shirley's *The Cardinal*
1641   Irish rebel; Star Chamber abolished
       Richard Brome's *A Jovial Crew*
1642   Outbreak of hostilities (English Civil Wars, 1642–9); Battle
       of Edgehill; Charles I leaves London; closure of London
       theatres by Act of Parliament

James Shirley's *The Sisters*

1645 New Model Army formed

1646 End of First Civil War

1647 Parliamentary Army occupies London; Charles I allies with Scots

1648 Second Civil War

1649 Execution of Charles I; establishment of English Commonwealth

Abbreviations and References

With such undervalued and under-studied dramatists as these, it is not always easy to find accessible modern editions of their plays. It is to be hoped that publishers will recognize the need for new editions in this area.

In the meantime I have used editions of the plays in single series for each dramatist for reasons of clarity, and have, where necessary, modernized spellings. For Massinger and Ford this does not pose too many difficulties – for Massinger I have employed *The Selected Plays of Philip Massinger*, edited by Colin Gibson (Cambridge: Cambridge University Press, 1978) and for Ford the recent World's Classics *'Tis Pity She's a Whore and Other Plays*, edited by Marion Lomax (Oxford: Oxford University Press, 1995). All the plays of Massinger and Ford studied in detail here are included in these editions, but for other plays in their canon please consult the Select Bibliography at the back of this book.

The dramatic corpus of James Shirley and Richard Brome is more problematic. In the case of both playwrights, complete works published in the nineteenth century are available in most scholarly libraries. These do not, however, provide line references for the plays. For consistency of reference, however, I have elected to use these editions for all the plays quoted here: for Shirley, the six-volume *Dramatic Works*, edited by W. Gifford and A. J. Dyce (London: J. Murray, 1833), and for Brome the three-volume *Dramatic Works*, edited by John Pearson (London: Pearson, 1873). Where, as in the case of Richard Brome, there are specific easily accessible recent scholarly editions of single plays, with line numbers, I have offered additional references in brackets after the quotations. This is relevant in the case of *The Antipodes* and *A Jovial Crew*, for which I have offered act, scene, and line references from

Ann Haaker's editions (see below under *Antipodes* and *Crew*). See the Select Bibliography at the back of this book for other useful publications of these plays.

Antipodes	Ann Haaker (ed.), *Richard Brome's 'The Antipodes'* (London: Arnold, 1968)
Brome	John Pearson (ed.), *Richard Brome: Dramatic Works*, 3 vols (London: Pearson, 1873)
Butler	Martin Butler, *Theatre and Crisis, 1632–42* (Cambridge: Cambridge University Press, 1984)
Clark	Ira Clark, *Professional Playwrights: Massinger, Ford, Shirley, and Brome* (Lexington, Ky.: University of Kentucky Press, 1992)
Crew	Ann Haaker (ed.), *Richard Brome's 'A Jovial Crew'* (London: Arnold, 1966)
Ford	Marion Lomax (ed.), *John Ford: 'Tis Pity She's a Whore and Other Plays* (Oxford: Oxford University Press, 1995)
Hill	Christopher Hill, *Puritanism and Revolution* (London: Mercury, 1962)
Hopkins	Lisa Hopkins, *John Ford's Political Theatre* (Manchester: Manchester University Press, 1994)
Howard	Douglas Howard (ed.), *Philip Massinger: A Critical Reassessment* (Cambridge: Cambridge University Press, 1985)
Jonson	C. H. Herford and Percy and Evelyn Simpson (eds), *Ben Jonson*, 11 vols (Oxford: Oxford University Press, 1925–52)
Massinger	Colin Gibson (ed.), *Selected Plays of Philip Massinger* (Cambridge: Cambridge University Press, 1978)
Neill	Michael Neill (ed.), *John Ford: Critical Re-Visions* (Cambridge: Cambridge University Press, 1988)
Shakespeare	Stephen Greenblatt *et al.* (eds), *The Norton Shakespeare* (London and New York: Norton, 1997)
Sharpe	Kevin Sharpe, *The Personal Rule of Charles I* (New Haven: Yale University Press, 1992)
Shirley	W. Gifford and A. J. Dyce (eds), *James Shirley: Dramatic Works*, 6 vols (London: J. Murray, 1833)
Smith	David L. Smith, Richard Strier and David Bevington (eds), *The Theatrical City: Culture, Theatre and*

	Politics in London 1576–1649 (Cambridge: Cambridge University Press, 1995)
Tomlinson	Sophie Tomlinson, '"She That Plays the King": Henrietta Maria and the Threat of the Actress in Caroline Culture', in Gordon McMullan and Jonathan Hope (eds), *The Politics of Tragicomedy* (London: Routledge, 1992), pp. 189–207
Traub	Valerie Traub, 'The (In)significance of "Lesbian" Desire in Early Modern England', in Susan Zimmermann (ed.), *Erotic Politics: Desire on the Renaissance Stage* (London: Routledge, 1992), pp. 150–69
Trussler	Simon Trussler (ed.), *James Shirley's 'Hyde Park'* (London: Methuen [RSC Programme/Text], 1987)
Veevers	Erica Veevers, *Images of Love and Religion: Queen Henrietta Maria and Court Entertainments* (Cambridge: Cambridge University Press, 1989)
Wymer	Rowland Wymer, *Webster and Ford* (London: Macmillan, 1995)

1

Caroline Drama and Dramatists

The reign of King Charles I did not officially end until 30 January 1649, when he was beheaded by the parliamentarian forces led by Generals Cromwell and Fairfax on a public scaffold erected, with tragic irony, in front of the Banqueting House, the Whitehall building he himself had some years earlier commissioned from the architect Inigo Jones. The poet Andrew Marvell's 'An Horatian Ode Upon Cromwell's Return from Ireland' describes the world-shattering event thus:

> He nothing common did, or mean,
> Upon the memorable Scene:
> > But with his keener Eye
> > The Axe's edge did try:
> Nor call'd the Gods with vulgar spight
> To vindicate his helpless Right,
> > But bow'd his comely Head
> > Down, as upon a Bed.

(ll. 57–64)

Civil war in England had broken out some seven years earlier, and it is more usually this date – 1642 – that is taken to mark the end of the so-called Caroline era that had begun with Charles's accession to the English throne upon the death of his father, James I, in 1625. Our focus in this book is on drama written during this reign – 1625–42 – by four of the period's most eminent public theatre dramatists: Philip Massinger, John Ford, James Shirley, and Richard Brome. Their dramatic 'reign' is generally held to have ended in 1642 with the outbreak of military hostilities between supporters of the king (the so-called royalists, or 'Cavaliers') and parliament (the roundheads, or

Puritans), and the attendant closure of the public theatres in London that same year.

'Cromwell and the Puritans' – a problematic category in itself – are often charged with responsibility for that closure, but the historical truth is rather more complex. The Puritans were, after all, scarcely in control in 1642 when Charles was still officially monarch of the realm. Moreover, the theatres were only closed for one season in the first instance, and more for reasons of public safety in wartime than because of any anti-theatrical political or theological ideology. It is true to say that the theatres were in London and that the city was itself ostensibly Parliamentarian and Puritan in its sympathies, and it is a fact that, subsequently, a number of the London playhouses were physically dismantled, timber by timber, by forces sympathetic to Cromwell. It is also a fact that public theatre was subsequently prohibited; but that is not to say that theatre did not continue in other guises (not least masque and the early forms of opera) during the time of the English republic, and as a result the closure of the theatres in 1642 should be read as a product of wartime necessity rather than any concerted campaign by Parliament. Nevertheless, in 1642 public theatre in England was temporarily halted, and not revived in full until the Restoration of the monarchy in 1660. By that time, of our four focus dramatists, only James Shirley was still alive, and he and his wife were to die in 1666 after a grim near-escape from the Great Fire of London. It is therefore up until 1642 and no further that our considerations of these dramatists' careers will carry us here.

Massinger, Ford, Shirley, and Brome were far from being the only dramatists of any significance in the Caroline period. Ben Jonson wrote several important plays between 1625 and his own death in 1637, including *The Staple of News* (1626), *The New Inn* (1629), *The Magnetic Lady* (1632), and *A Tale of a Tub* (1633). John Fletcher also wrote many interesting plays, both singly and collaboratively. Types of drama and entertainment other than straight plays were also produced, including the masques of William Davenant and the 'secular masque' of John Milton, *A Mask Presented at Ludlow Castle*, better known as *Comus* (1634). There was also a spate of dramas commissioned specifically for court performance, in particular the pastorals and Neoplatonic plays written for and performed by Charles's French wife,

Queen Henrietta Maria, from 1626 onwards.

Our concern here, though, will be with public-theatre dramatists and with single-authored texts. This is not to devalue collaborative literary productions, which were, after all, considerable in this period, but it is to acknowledge that an account of collaborative writing would require a different kind of approach and a different kind of book to the one being attempted here. Massinger, Ford, Shirley, and Brome are all closely identified with the period in hand. Although Massinger was already a playwright of some significance, his early works were largely collaborative efforts, many co-written with John Fletcher: his major sole-authored works were all produced during the Caroline reign. Prior to the 1620s John Ford wrote only poetry and collaborative drama; and both Shirley and Brome are Caroline dramatists to the core.

Our focus, then, is with dramatists who wrote for a variety of commercial theatre playhouses between 1625 and 1642. At that time the large open-air amphitheatre playhouses located south of the River Thames in the so-called 'Liberties' area, in which William Shakespeare had made his name, were still operating – the Globe, the Hope, the Rose, the Swan – but the emphasis had by this time shifted to the indoor, more expensive hall-playhouses within the city of London proper: in particular the Blackfriars (home of Shakespeare's former company, the King's Men) and the newly erected Cockpit (also known as the Phoenix) and Salisbury Court theatres. This geographical and cultural shift to the potentially more élite domains of the hall playhouses has led to the historical cliché that in the Caroline era theatre became more exclusive and, by implication, more closely allied to the court and its royalist politics. Martin Butler's seminal book, *Theatre and Crisis, 1632–42* (1984), has done much to query this assumption, suggesting that the public playhouses remained sites of opposition and critique in the Caroline period, much as they had been in the Jacobean. The sense of an increasing theatrical influence deriving from the court has also led to charges of visual and moral decadence being laid against plays written by these dramatists (Ford has been a particular victim of such readings, and Shirley has been frequently dismissed as a court propagandist). Their tragicomic and romantic plotlines have been stressed as proof that they offered

3

escapism from political realities in the decade leading up to civil war. It has been argued that what these plays constituted was a royalist retreat into aesthetic indulgence in the face of social and political tensions and decline. Books published as late as the 1970s were dismissing the drama of this period as 'frivolous' and unworthy of discussion.

In this book, and following in Butler's wake, I want to offer a different possibility for readings of Caroline drama, and to suggest that these plays rarely represent escapist indulgences and are more often than not direct engagements with social, political, and indeed theatrical realities in the moment in which they were produced. I want to offer more nuanced and complex portraits of the four dramatists who are my major concern, and I hope in turn to inspire readers to familiarize themselves with the rich repertoire of plays to which they contributed. It is too often a fact that theatre histories of the seventeenth century gloss over the Caroline period, either ignoring it completely or presenting it as a period of aberration, of a falling-off from the high aesthetic achievements of the Elizabethan and Jacobean eras, or as a poor precursor of Restoration drama. In a book of this size and scope I can only ever offer a taste of what Caroline drama has to offer: it is to be hoped that readers will find areas of future interest for themselves.

I have organized the following four chapters of the book under general headings in order to offer certain (but by no means exclusive) ways of reading the plays highlighted. Chapter 2, 'Court and Kingship', therefore elaborates on plays that deal with courtly settings and ideas of monarchy and rule. The court masque and its influence on the visual splendour and tableaux of Caroline theatre writing is considered here. Chapter 3 looks at the particular influence that Henrietta Maria's theatrical patronage had on public-theatre plays and the debate around women and acting that was raging in the late 1620s and 1630s. Chapter 4, 'City and Town', examines the inheritance from Jonsonian city comedy and the particular brand of 'town' drama that developed in the 1630s, and Chapter 5 moves outside the town to explore 'Country and Community', taking us right up to 1642 and the conditions of theatre on the eve of the civil wars. First, however, it would be as well to familiarize ourselves with the dramatists whose work we will be interrogating in the

4

process. Philip Massinger was born in Salisbury in 1583. He was actively writing for the stage as early as the 1610s, but it was only in the 1620s that he began to write alone. *The Maid of Honour* (?1621–2) is his earliest unaided work. In the same year he wrote his Italianate tragedy *The Duke of Milan*, and in 1624 *The Unnatural Combat*. These last two plays were written for and performed by the King's Men, the adult male theatre company attached to the Globe and the Blackfriars theatres, and after 1626 (the time when we are most engaged with Massinger's career in this book) Massinger wrote solely for this company. Between 1624 and 1626 he authored a number of other playtexts, for some of which we only have fragmentary remains, including comedies such as *The Parliament of Love* in 1624 and *A New Way to Pay Old Debts* in 1625. The latter play is central to the discussion of country communities in Chapter 5 of this book. In many respects Massinger's writing for the theatre came into its own following John Fletcher's death from plague in 1625, also, of course, the year of Charles I's accession. For the King's Men he wrote his tragedy *The Roman Actor* (1626), which we examine in detail in Chapter 2, *The Picture* (1629), *Believe As You List* (1631), *The Emperor of the East* (1631), his city comedy *The City Madam* (1632) – see Chapter 4 – and, amongst other plays, *The Bashful Lover* in 1636. Massinger died in 1640, but it was in the late 1620s and early 1630s that he had his heyday. His style is very wordy, and is frequently described as either eloquent or long-winded. He is also quite a repetitious writer, borrowing ideas and references both from other playwrights and from his own plays. Neither of these facts are necessarily negatives, as the exploration of the language of Caroline drama towards the end of this chapter will indicate.

Both *A New Way to Pay Old Debts* and *The City Madam* are strongly influenced by Jonsonian city comedy, and *The Roman Actor* by Jonsonian tragedy. *The Duke of Milan* and *The Picture* concern themselves with besotted rulers. However, in discussing Massinger's intertextuality we should not ignore the influence he had on other playwrights. *A New Way to Pay Old Debts,* itself in some ways a rewriting of Thomas Middleton's earlier *A Trick to Catch the Old One* (1605), heavily shaped Ben Jonson's *The New Inn*, and *The Roman Actor* with its intense metatheatricality set a certain tone for subsequent Caroline tragic drama. Like all the dramatists under discussion here, Massinger tried his hand at many genres: comedy, tragedy, tragicomedy, romance, and satire, to name a few.

John Ford is most renowned today for his tragedies, in particular 'Tis Pity She's a Whore (c.1630) and The Broken Heart (c.1629), both of which are frequently staged in the modern theatre and both of which are discussed in detail here (see Chapter 2). In the late twentieth century the French theorist of theatre, Antonin Artaud, chose 'Tis Pity She's a Whore to exemplify his notion of the 'Theatre of Cruelty' (Clark, 82), and both the film director Peter Greenaway (talking about his controversial movie The Cook, the Thief, His Wife, and her Lover) and the novelist Angela Carter (in a short story in her Old World Ghosts and New World Wonders collection) have acknowledged his influence. Ford's baroque, intensely visual and frequently violent plays are often seen as curiously paradigmatic of Caroline artistic decadence and yet they owe their own debts to Jacobean tragedies by John Webster and Thomas Middleton. 'Tis Pity She's a Whore is in many respects a grotesque rewriting of Romeo and Juliet and Middleton's own balcony-obsessed city comedy Women Beware Women (1621). Ford also wrote romantic tragicomedies, one of which, the 1628 The Lover's Melancholy, is discussed in Chapter 3.

Born in Devon in 1586, Ford wrote at least eleven independently authored plays, of which eight are extant. The first of these extant texts is The Lover's Melancholy (1628). Of his earlier collaborative drama, the best-known is probably The Witch of Edmonton, which he co-authored with William Rowley and Thomas Dekker in 1621. Prior to that he is better known as a poet and pamphleteer. In his early days as a dramatist he wrote largely for the King's Men at the Blackfriars (plays of this period include The Lover's Melancholy and The Broken Heart), but after that date his plays are linked to Christopher Beeston's company, the Queen's Men, at the Cockpit Theatre. After 'Tis Pity She's a Whore in 1630 he wrote his historical drama Perkin Warbeck (1632–4): both of these plays are examined in Chapter 2. Later plays include The Fancies Chaste and Noble and The Lady's Trial in 1638. We do not know when Ford died, but he disappears from public view in 1639. What has partly defined his drama for the twentieth century are his incredibly self-willed, if ultimately defeated, heroines: Eroclea in *The Lover's Melancholy* (the only one of his female protagonists who survives to the end of the play, and a kind of conscious reworking of the Shakespearean heroine), Penthea and Calantha in *The Broken Heart*, Annabella in *'Tis Pity She's a Whore*, and Katherine Gordon in *Perkin Warbeck*, to name but a few. In this respect the Ford canon can be compared to that of James Shirley.

James Shirley lived a long and varied life. Born in London in 1596, he went to the Merchant Taylor's School and from thence to Oxford. His first publication was a poem, 'Echo and Narcissus', in 1618. At around that time he converted to Catholicism and married his first wife. Appositely enough for us, it was in 1625 that his theatre career began in earnest. His first extant play, *Love Tricks; or, The School of Compliment*, was performed by Beeston's company (formerly the Lady Elizabeth's Men, but now reforming itself as Queen Henrietta Maria's Men on Charles I's marriage and accession) at the Cockpit that year. In 1626 he wrote a tragedy, *The Maid's Revenge*, and a comedy, *The Wedding* (for the publication of which Ford wrote a dedicatory verse). Shirley was prolific during the following decade authoring comedies, tragedies, historical drama, and tragicomic romances such as *The Grateful Servant* (1629), *The Traitor* (1631), *Love's Cruelty* (1631), *The Arcadia* (1632 – a reworking of Sir Philip Sidney's Elizabethan prose romance), and *The Lady of Pleasure* (1635). In 1637 the London theatres were closed due to a plague epidemic, and Shirley travelled to Ireland, directing plays in Dublin, including a successful production of Jonson's *The Alchemist*, and whilst there he wrote the original drama *St Patrick's for Ireland*. He returned to London following Massinger's death in 1640 to become chief dramatist for the King's Men at the Blackfriars, writing several more plays before the 1642 closure of the theatres. These plays included *The Country Captain*, which he co-wrote with William Cavendish, Earl of Newcastle, and the Italianate tragedy *The Cardinal*.

Shirley's links with the court and the aristocracy were considerable throughout his career. In 1634 he gained membership of one of the Inns of Court in London, and the records at Gray's Inn describe him as 'one of the valets of the chamber of Queen Henrietta Maria': this association, as we shall see in Chapter 3, had a considerable degree of influence on his drama.

7

Shirley's association with Cavendish extended into the civil war when he served in Newcastle's company for a time, eventually retiring into semi-obscurity as a schoolmaster. He continued to publish poetry and masques throughout the 1640s and 1650s, but few of these are known to have been performed. At some point he remarried, and both he and his second wife Frances died soon after fleeing the Great Fire of London.

We have space to look at only a selection of Shirley's plays here, and they have been chosen to exemplify particular aspects of his canon. *Hyde Park* (1632), which was performed by the Royal Shakespeare Company as recently as 1987, is a perfect example of his penchant for town subjects. *The Bird in a Cage* represents his controversial intervention in the debate about women and theatre in 1633, and *The Sisters* is a so-called 'vagabond play' written and performed on the cusp of the first civil war. Like Ford, Shirley's female protagonists are of particular interest, as is his treatment of women's acting in plays such as *The Bird in a Cage*. Whilst these sympathies do identify him with the feminocentric (and Catholic) coterie surrounding Henrietta Maria at court, his plays are seen to be complex and often ambiguous interventions into debates of the time, the 'courtly' aspects of his drama not necessarily being conservative or reactionary gestures.

Richard Brome is the one Caroline dramatist who has been viewed as standing outside the decadent circle of the court, although, like Ford and Shirley, he dedicates his plays to significant aristocrats, among them William Cavendish. Brome's popular and populist plays have gained considerable academic interest in recent years, and there has even been one performance, the Royal Shakespeare Company production of *A Jovial Crew* in 1992. It must be added, however, that the RSC felt the need to rewrite Brome in order to stage him, further proof if it were needed of the poor regard in which Caroline drama is held. Brome is, of course, also of interest because of his intimate associations with Ben Jonson, whose influence on all the dramatists examined here was considerable and extensive. For a time he was a servant in Jonson's household, where he obviously also gained his dramatic apprenticeship: indeed, the first mention of him after his birth in 1590 is in the Induction to Jonson's 1614 *Bartholomew Fair*, which describes 'Master Brome, behind the arras' (Jonson, VI: Induction, l. 8). Some suggest that he is the Brome who co-authored a play called *A Fault in Friendship* with one 'Young Johnson' which was entered in the Stationers' Register in 1623, but Jonson specialists consider this too speculative to be of account. What is certain is that by 1628 he was a player in the Queen of Bohemia's company, and that by 1629 single-authored plays by him were being entered on the register, including in that year *The City Wit* and *The Northern Lass*, in 1632 *The Novella* and *The Weeding of Covent Garden*, in 1635 *The Sparagus Garden* and *The New Academy*, in 1636 *The Queen and Concubine*, in 1637 *The English Moor*, in 1638 *The Antipodes*, in 1639 *A Mad Couple Well-Matched* (adapted for the Restoration Stage by the female professional playwright, Aphra Behn), and in 1641 *A Jovial Crew*. Nothing is known of Brome after the outbreak of the civil wars, but in 1653 a printing of his plays records him as deceased. His impressive dramatic canon indicates his generic variety: the list includes tragedies, comedies, and masque-influenced and popular plays. He also wrote a number of collaborative dramas, although many are now lost; one of the most significant was the Caroline witchcraft play *The Late Lancashire Witches* written with Thomas Heywood in 1634. Once again we can only look at a small selection of Brome's works here, and again the choice is deliberately focused. Chapter 4 considers several of his London-based plays, particularly their focus on family and politics and, indeed, family politics: plays such as *The Weeding of Covent Garden*, *The Sparagus Garden*, and *The Antipodes*. Chapter 5 looks in detail at the community politics of *A Jovial Crew* and its poignant position, along with Shirley's *The Sisters*, as one of the last plays staged in the English public theatres before the civil wars of 1642–9.

The individual chapters of this book are therefore explicitly concerned with the construction and political meanings of these plays; but this is not to underestimate or even to sideline their linguistic and poetic richness. The strengths and diversity of the language of Elizabethan and Jacobean drama have been well-rehearsed, not least through studies of Shakespearean verse. However, in the same way that the subject-matter and ethical concerns of Caroline drama have been dismissed as being 'decadent' and purely aesthetic, so its language has been charged with a looseness both of tone and prosody in comparison with that in the work of its dramatic predecessors such as Shakespeare and Jonson. Of course, as we shall discover at various points in this book, Jonson was still a significant writer in the 1620s and 1630s and an important influence on both Brome and Shirley, so that separation of cultural discourses is in itself unsustainable. The Jacobean readily shades into the Caroline, and I would argue that similar energies, both of expression and image, exist in the plays produced in the later period.

Massinger's language has been a focus for much critical debate. In the late nineteenth century Edmund Gosse dismissed it as being 'uniform and humdrum' and lacking in lyricism. T. S. Eliot echoed this sense of the plainness of Massinger's dramatic discourse in his own early twentieth-century account (Howard, 9). Neither of these views survives a sustained application to the plays themselves. The language to be found there is rich in imagery and local relevance, diverse in its structures and syntax, and frequently used to make differentiations between characters on either an emotional or intellectual level or in terms of their social status within the communities of the plays.

The Roman Actor, for example, is a theatrical *tour de force* with no fewer than four inset plays in the course of its plotline, each with their own integral series of images and verbal pictures (Howard, 25). In Act III the actor Paris performs the role of Iphis, a despairing lover, who makes appeals to Cupid so convincingly that the Emperor's mistress Domitia falls in love with the character he plays:

> Does he not act it rarely?
> Observe with what a feeling he delivers
> His orisons to Cupid; I am rapt with it.

(Massinger, III. ii. 175–7)

Massinger's is above all a highly theatrical and theatrically self-conscious language. He is aware of language's power to entice and to seduce, as well as to entertain.

It is command of language that invests Sir Giles Overreach with much of his social and theatrical energy and influence in *A New Way to Pay Old Debts*. Preparing for a banquet by means of which he hopes to further his standing in the local Nottinghamshire community, he demands: 'Spare for no cost; let my dressers crack with the weight| Of curious viands' (III. ii. 1–2).

He is similarly self-assertive – a tone achieved in part through use of the imperative tense, in part through the thrusting stressed monosyllables of his lines – before his daughter Margaret, through whose marriage he hopes to gain both wealth and title:

> Virgin me no virgins!
> I must have you lose that name, or you lose me.
> I will have you private – start not – I say private,
> If thou art my true daughter, not a bastard,
> Thou wilt venture alone with one man, though he came
> Like Jupiter to Semele, and come off too.
> And therefore when he kisses you, kiss close.

> (III. ii. 112–18)

Overreach shuns the lessons and counsel of myth-making and will write his life-text as he wishes. Something similar might be said of the hypocritical Luke Frugal in *The City Madam*, another figure of greed and ambition whose personality traits can be traced through the operations of his speeches. A long soliloquy at III. iii reveals a mind driven into the realm of fantasy by the wealth he supposes he has inherited. Elsewhere he is more conniving, beguiling his brother's wife and daughters with promises of courtly greatness. His is highly polysyllabic language, full of rich images and almost Marlovian qualities of excess, as exemplified by his chastizing of the women's fondness for fashion:

> The reverend hood cast off, your borrow'd hair,
> Powder'd and curl'd, was by your dresser's art
> Form'd like a coronet, hang'd with diamonds,
> And the richest orient pearl;

> (IV. iv. 103–6)

This might be a Volpone seducing Celia: the tropes are comparable. Were Gosse's criticisms of Massinger's language true we might expect a similarity of style between an Overreach and a Luke Frugal; instead, there is huge diversity and difference in the language accorded to characters in Massinger's plays, even within the same play.

One of the charges Gosse also laid against Massinger was the prose-like qualities of his verse, suggesting that its metricality, such as it was, was perfunctory rather than performative of function. The variation of stress in Overreach's and Frugal's speeches serves to question this account of the musicality or otherwise of Caroline poetry. Whilst there may have been some loosening of the strict conventions of Stuart verse-speaking, the use of stress and rhyme remains integral to the effect. John Ford is no exception to this rule, although he is perhaps, imagistically speaking, even more striking than Massinger. Both playwrights are painters of vivid verbal pictures. In the fourth act of Ford's *The Broken Heart* Ithocles confesses his love for Princess Calantha. It is an affection that transgresses social boundaries and so, in articulating this transgressive emotion, Ithocles's language starts to break out of the strict containment of the iambic pentameter line:

> In anger let him part; for could his breath,
> Like whirlwinds, toss such servile slaves as lick
> The dust his footsteps print into a vapour,
> It durst not stir a hair of mine. It should not;
> I'd rend it up by th'roots first. To be anything
> Calantha smiles on is to be a blessing
> More sacred than a petty-prince of Argos
> Can wish to equal, or in worth or title.

> (Ford, IV. i. 61–8)

Words like 'vapour', 'anything', and 'blessing' reach out beyond the end-stressed pentameter and dissolve into the unstressed world of vain hopes and social impossibilities. Ithocles will only marry Calantha as a corpse in this bleak drama. Armostes seems to note the dangerous portent of Ithocles's scansion here:

> Contain yourself, my lord. Ixion, aiming
> To embrace Juno, bosomed but a cloud,
> And begat centaurs.

> (IV i. 69–71)

Like Massinger's, Ford's language is steeped in images and tales derived from classical mythology, but Colin Gibson has high-lighted a particular investment in Ford's language in the 'poetry of death' (Neill, 55). One striking example comes in the Friar's counsel to Annabella in *'Tis Pity She's a Whore* over the hellish consequences of her transgressive love, an incestuous relationship with her twin brother Giovanni:

Ay, you are wretched, miserably wretched,

Almost condemned alive. There is a place –
List daughter – in a black and hollow vault,
Where day is never seen; there shines no sun,
But flaming horror of consuming fires;
A lightless sulphur, choked with smoky fogs
Of an infected darkness. In this place
Dwell many thousand thousand sundry sorts
Of never-dying deaths: there, damned souls
Roar without pity; there, are gluttons fed
With toads and adders; there is burning oil
Poured down the drunkard's throat; the usurer
Is forced to sup whole draughts of molten gold;
There is the murderer forever stabbed,
Yet can he never die; there lies the wanton
On racks of burning steel, whiles in his soul
He feels the torment of his raging lust.

(III. vi. 6–23)

The language and the images are as unrelenting as Ford's depiction of corrupted societies in his tragedies.

Shirley and Brome, perhaps in part because more inclined to the comic or tragicomic modes, more obviously resist the lengthy soliloquies of Elizabethan and Stuart drama which Massinger and Ford so clearly retain. An impression of one of their plays is more likely to be of lively dialogues between characters in which the differentiations of discourse serve to spark off tensions and conflicts within the context of the exchange. The varied stage communities of plays such as Shirley's *Hyde Park* or Brome's *The Weeding of Covent Garden* are cases in point. The third and fourth acts of *Hyde Park* which take place within the park itself are composed of short intersecting speeches between different pairs or groups. The pace is quick and the tone light, although this is not to underestimate Shirley's creative skills in composing the scenes in this manner. The metrical rhythms are more speech-like, not because of lack of skill on the part of the dramatist but because a more conversational tone is being sought. The poeticized language of love and romance is consistently challenged and deconstructed by the exchanges of this play, be it through Carol's assertive, feminocentric rejection of the clichéd wooing of her suitors or Julietta's rank-driven refusal to believe the worst of Lord Bonvile's seductive speeches:

BONVILE.   Lady, you are welcome to the spring; the Park

> Looks fresher to salute you: how the birds
> On every tree sing, with more cheerfulness
> At your access, as if they prophesied
> Nature would die, and resign her providence
> To you, fit only to succeed her!

JULIETTA.   You express
> A master of all compliment; I have
> Nothing but plain humility, my lord to answer you . . .
> It seems your lordship speaks to one you know not.

BONVILE.   But I desire to know you better, lady.
JULIETTA.   Better I should desire, my lord.

(Shirley, II, III. i. pp. 492–3)

Intriguingly, it is women who are Shirley's plain speakers, and this confirms an empathy with women in his plays that I want to trace in more detail in later chapters.

Both Shirley and Brome, however, like Massinger and Ford, are alert to the possibilities of theatrical and theatricalized poetry. Both have plays of their own with inset dramas: Shirley's *The Bird in a Cage*, where a group of women from different sectors of society perform the story of Jupiter and Danaë, and Brome's *The Antipodes*, where Peregrine is convinced by the performance of Lord Letoy's actors that he has travelled to a foreign land, and *A Jovial Crew*, where the beggars' masque provides a microcosm of that play's wider lessons and message. Each playwright is capable of shifts of tones and register that enable an audience to comprehend the different imaginative worlds being entered at any given time. Both consciously resist the overblown or melodramatic in their speeches, a point made clear by Lord Letoy's Hamlet-like instructions to the players in *The Antipodes*:

> Trouble not you your head with my conceit,
> But mind your part. Let me not see you act now
> In your scholastic way you brought to town wi'ye,
> With seesaw sack a down, like a sawyer;
> Nor in a comic scene play *Hercules Furens*,
> Tearing your throat to split the audient's ears.
> And you, sir, you had got a trick of late
> Of holding out your bum in a set speech,
> Your fingers fibulating on your breast
> As if your buttons or your band-strings were
> Helps to your memory . . .

14

I'll none of these absurdities in my house,
But words and actions so married together
That shall strike harmony in the ears and eyes
Of the severest, if judicious, critics.

(Brome, III, II. ii. p. 259; Antipodes II. ii. 15–25, 34–7)

'Words and actions married together' may provide us with a kind of manifesto for Caroline drama. There is social realism of a kind being aimed for here, and perhaps the loosening of poetic convention by these plays could be seen as an intrinsic part of that project. Brome, in *A Jovial Crew* in particular, lays great store by the language of the common people. However, this is not necessarily a Caroline innovation: it links, rather, to those all-important Jonsonian precedents I have been mentioning. These vibrant stage communities with all their slang and colloquialisms and rich idioms continue a tradition established as early as the 1610s and plays such as *The Alchemist* and *Bartholomew Fair*. The language of Caroline drama has its own rich cadences, but that should not prevent us recognizing its continuities with Elizabethan and Jacobean forebears.

I can only offer a brief survey here of the depth and possibility of a linguistic exploration of the work of Massinger, Ford, Shirley, and Brome; and, in the same way, this book makes no claims to being a comprehensive account of either Caroline drama or its four focus dramatists. It is intended as an introduction, one that will hopefully encourage greater interest in this period, so fascinating in terms of its drama and its politics, and that will inspire readers and students to carve out paths for themselves through the period and its literary output. Similarly, the subject areas offered here for consideration are by no means the only possible readings of the plays discussed: they are intended as interesting windows on the complex and sometimes obscured architecture, aesthetic, social, and political, of this neglected moment of cultural history. If every reader picks up at least one Caroline play to read as a result, then this writer will have done her work.

2

Court and Kingship

In 1625 Charles I succeeded his late father, James I, as King of England. The intended ceremony and celebrations to mark Charles's coronation did not, however, take place in 1625. They were postponed, partly due to plague, but largely due to financial difficulties, until the following year. Charles's first opportunity as king for self-presentation was temporarily thwarted, and the belated and therefore rather anachronistic nature of the coronation ceremony when it did occur (it was considerably downscaled) seemed to colour popular attitudes towards his subsequent court theatricals and artistic and aesthetic pursuits during the rest of the reign. The popular perception was of their vast, and by implication unnecessary, expense (a single performance could cost as much as £3,000), their detachment from the concerns of Charles's subjects and the realm, and their innate élitism. In some respects they were all viewed, like that delayed and downsized coronation, as being far from timely occurrences.

Charles was a great collector of art and sculpture, a tendency which had asserted itself as early as 1626. Among the artists he favoured were Rubens, Van Dyck, and Mantegna, all of whom created pictures that celebrated absolute power and concepts of divine monarchy. Charles's belief in the divine sanctioning of monarchy clearly influenced his taste in art and aesthetics. He made major investments in courtly depictions and self-representations, in pictures to be read in terms of power or at least the 'illusion of power'. One of his most significant purchases for his collection was Andrea Mantegna's visual paean to absolutism, 'The Triumphs of Caesar', and in 1632 Charles himself performed as Caesar, leading captive kings (an image familiar from the Mantegna paintings) in Aurelian Townshend's Roman masque, *Albion's Triumph*.

In terms of theatre proper, the most obvious ways in which Charles and his Queen, Henrietta Maria, the sister of the French monarch, used theatre at the court to reinforce and perpetuate their power was through the genre of the court masque, a form that had been employed to similar purpose by Charles's father and his late brother (Prince Henry, the initial heir to James's throne, who had died so suddenly in 1612). To a certain extent the masque had been developed in its present form by Charles's mother, Anne of Denmark, in the earlier part of the century, through her commissions of Ben Jonson and Inigo Jones to stage such controversial masques as the *Masque of Blackness* (1605) and the *Masque of Queens* (1609), for the purpose of which Jonson credited the queen herself with the invention of the antimasque prelude to the masquing proper. In that masque the antimasque involved witches, a subversive female image in itself.

The masque was a piece of court theatre in which the court itself participated as patrons, commissioners, and indeed performers. It involved both spoken and gestural theatre, what we more commonly term 'drama', but also music, dance, and spectacular visuals in a kind of 'total theatre' in which each part was integral to the whole. The prime exponents of the Jacobean court masques were Jonson and Jones, who collaborated on productions from 1605 onwards; but other masque writers included Thomas Middleton, George Chapman, and Samuel Daniel. Many of the costume and elaborate stage designs that Jones developed to coincide with Jonson's masque texts are extant today and give us some idea of the splendour of the performances. The permanence of these printed remains of the masques, Jonson's scripts, carefully edited for publication in his 1616 folio *Works*, and Jones's colourful designs, should not, however, detract us from appreciating the essentially temporary and ephemeral nature of the masque performance. These 'shows' usually took place on a single evening, during the so-called Christmas season at court which usually ran until Shrovetide (the beginning of Lent), and were highly resonant in terms of their cultural moment. They were invariably performed, at least in part, by important figures of the day, including the queen herself on a number of occasions. It is this vivid but brief theatrical experience that was the Caroline inheritance so far as the masque was concerned.

There has been considerable debate as to the political significance or otherwise of these topical masque texts. Some critics have viewed the masque form as quintessentially royalist, employed by the court to enforce and endorse its position of power. Others have noted a more critical, even subversive, tone to some of the Jonsonian masque-texts, tracing ways in which the occasions were employed to counsel the monarch and his court. Court theatre could then be ambivalent in its effect upon the watching audiences, which were made up of courtiers who would themselves have been a diverse mixture of those supportive of, and those involved in factions against, the King. Court theatre in its often feminocentric origins could also be, potentially at least, subversive of patriarchal power (and by extension the paternalistic position of the King), and Queen Anne has been credited with purposes of this nature in her commissioning of masques from Jonson and others. This aspect of the masque was another Caroline inheritance, and one which Charles's wife, Henrietta Maria, was not averse to exploiting, as we shall see in Chapter 3.

None of the dramatists with which we are concerned actually wrote court masques in the Caroline period, although James Shirley authored masques such as the 1634 *The Triumph of Peace* for other venues such as the London Inns of Court which were presented to the court; but this is not to say that they were not influenced by or seen to comment on court theatre as a result. Philip Massinger, James Shirley, John Ford, and Richard Brome all include versions or appropriations of court masques within the context of their public theatre plays. Often this is done for sheer dramatic effect. The masque, as we have stated, was visually spectacular, and its use of both court performers and professional actors quite self-consciously blurred the boundary line between reality and fiction, undoubtedly a theme of interest in the metatheatrical texts of these playwrights. But the Caroline dramatists also seem to have recognized in the masque a means of making indirect (and therefore safer) comment on events at court: it is metadrama with a distinctly political edge, and may well be court-aimed in its focus. In order to explore these observations in greater detail I intend in this chapter to focus on a series of plays that represent courts and courtly settings on the public stage and which use the masque form to capture the essence of courtly

18

institutions. Whilst none depicts a 'real' Caroline court, it will be seen that the alternative courts of Ancient Rome, as in Massinger's *The Roman Actor*, of Sparta, in John Ford's *The Broken Heart*, and of Tudor England in *Perkin Warbeck* are employed to highlight both parallels with and differences to the contemporary situation in 1620s and 1630s England.

The Roman Actor will be explored in the context of debates about appearance and reality that seemed to cluster around the self-conscious Caroline court, with particular attention paid to Massinger's integral ruminations on the power of theatre. The performance of monarchy and the court at large is also seen to be a driving concern of Ford's *Perkin Warbeck*, with its story of a pretender to the throne of England, and his relentless tragedy *The Broken Heart*, with its visual and active investment in courtly rituals and ceremonies. All these plays are engaged with questions of power and, in particular, patriarchal power, and this understanding is used to produce a reading of Ford's most famous tragedy, *'Tis Pity She's a Whore*, which, although it is less overtly a court play in terms of its setting, connects in a very real sense with the concerns about authority and social injustice evidenced by these other dramas.

Philip Massinger's *The Roman Actor* was written and first performed in 1626, that is to say, in the initial years of Charles I's reign. It was not uncommon in the Renaissance for dramatists to use the early years of any monarch to try, through their work, to offer advice and guidance that might contribute to and inform the nature and political and social objectives of that reign. Ben Jonson's *Sejanus, His Fall*, written in 1603 in the first year of the reign of Charles's father, is a case in point. Jonson used his play, set in Ancient Rome under the tyrannical rule of Emperor Tiberius, to instruct James I in the ways not to behave, and even included a plea for freedom of speech to be allowed to writers in the central trial lament of the persecuted historian Cordus. Cordus's books, which in the admiration they express for republicans such as Brutus and Cassius (who assassinated Julius Caesar) implicitly challenge imperial rule, are ordered to be burned. It is to be remembered that just four years before Jonson's play, William Shakespeare had written the play *Julius Caesar* about these events.

Massinger uses *Sejanus* and, indeed, precise events in Jonson's play such as the trial of Cordus, as a shaping text for his own tragic drama set in Ancient Rome. *The Roman Actor* takes place during the rule of the cruel and tyrannical Emperor Domitian (51–96 AD) and includes the onstage trial, not of a writer, but this time of theatre itself, in the form of a representative actor, the highly articulate Paris, who finds himself speaking in his own defence in I. iii.

Domitian would have been well-known to early modern audiences, as he is today, as the enthusiastic patron of bloody sports and cruel public theatre staged at his 'Circus', the outline of which can still be seen in modern Rome. This, then, is a play essentially concerned with political tyranny, with cruel and arbitrary absolutism, with the transforming power of theatre amidst tyranny, and with the use and abuse of theatre by those in power.

Massinger is not by any means charging Charles with tyranny, or even with the potential for it, but he is counselling the new monarch in ways not to govern, just as Ben Jonson had done his royal father before him. Massinger also defends his right to do this: this is a self-referential play that debates the use of censorship by those in government to silence those who criticize or oppose their way of rule. In an eloquent speech Paris stresses the cathartic power of theatre as a direct response to charges that his work corrupts spectators:

> We show no arts of Lydian pandarism,
> Corinthian poisons, Persian flatteries,
> But mulcted so in the conclusion that
> Even those spectators that were so inclin'd
> Go home chang'd men.

(Massinger, I. iii. 102–6)

Domitian is a lover of theatre, it seems, but only theatre that serves his personal purposes, purposes which we rapidly come to regard as both morally and sexually decadent. His is to be a theatre of 'soft delights', although we also perceive this to be a theatre of hidden cruelty, as he pretends mercy to certain accused people, only to execute them when they least expect it. This occurs early in the play in Domitian's feigning of friendship to Lamia – husband to Domitian's mistress, Domitia – only, with a sense of cruel thrill, to order the relieved man's beheading, and it is repeated in Act IV with the execution of Paris in the midst of a play in which Domitian has insisted on performing. Theatre is seen less as a source of corruption than as corrupted in its purposes by the abuses of tyrannical government.

Domitian's 'performances' contribute to a general blurring of truth and fiction in the play. So embedded have the theatrical commissions become in the performance of Domitian's power at court that his mistress Domitia can no longer distinguish between the two worlds of Rome and the stage. As a consequence she develops an uncontrollable passion for Paris in performance – an audience response that effectively condemns the actor to death.

Masques trod a similarly fine line between truth and performance, featuring as they did so many 'real-life' performers and so many references to the actual situation at court. Ben Jonson was not suggesting in any way in *Sejanus* that James I was akin to the Emperor Tiberius; nor is Massinger likening Charles I and Domitian in *The Roman Actor*. Both dramatists were, however, voicing a plea for leniency and tolerance, for an openness to critique on the part of the monarchy, rather than a silencing of all opponents. In truth, respect for the institution of royalty is implicit in Massinger's text: even after Domitian has been killed by a group of revengers, the Roman tribunes who had attempted to counsel him towards better government are troubled by the slaying of a 'prince' (the language of monarchy is quite deliberately employed in the play). Good government, not republican, non-monarchical government is the purpose of the counsel here. Nevertheless it does seem to indicate that plays that featured court settings at this time were inviting parallels with the contemporary situation, if not proffering a clumsy allegory of the same.

Power and the ability to perform are explicitly connected in Massinger's play, as they were in the political advice tracts written by the Italian Renaissance political theorist, Niccolò Machiavelli. John Ford also relates the two in his 1634 history play, *Perkin Warbeck*, the story of an impostor-king who challenges the rule of the Tudor monarch, Henry VII. Henry is susceptible to such suggestions because in the past, as the Duke of Richmond, he claimed the throne by might when he slew the villainous Richard III at the Battle of Bosworth (again the subject of a Shakespearean play). The 'counterfeit king' Perkin Warbeck presents himself as one of the two sons of Edward IV believed slain by Richard in the Tower of London as a young boy, and wins European and, indeed, Scottish support (in the shape of James IV) for his cause. The distinction between royalty and the performance of royalty is once again dangerously blurred.

History plays were by no means as fashionable a genre in the 1630s as they had been in the 1590s when Shakespeare had staged the majority of his ventures into the realm of the recent British past. The critic Lisa Hopkins, however, in her book *John Ford's Political Theatre* (1994), has suggested a topical resonance for Ford's play equal to that I have identified for Massinger's *The Roman Actor*, seeing in it an endorsement of the Tudor line and suggesting that the Tudor monarchs (Henry VII, Henry VIII, and Elizabeth I) are being put forward as models for Charles to follow, rather than his Stuart forebears (figured in the machinatory and shifting behaviour of James IV) (Hopkins, 39–71). Whether this is a play engaged with the question of succession or not, the problematic link it forms between the court's presentation of itself to the people and the deceptive and counterfeit nature of theatre should not be underestimated as offering its own mode of counsel to Charles I. By 1634 Charles had already ruled for some five years without summoning a parliament, and this was beginning to provoke considerable constitutional debate about the accountability of the King to his elected parliament, a debate that would ultimately contribute to the civil wars of the following decade. He would rule without a parliament for a further six years, a period that came to be known as the 'Personal Rule' (1629–40); and the theatre produced in that time can be seen as in some sense providing an alternative arena for debate whilst the chambers of the Houses of the Commons and the Lords remained so decidedly shut. There is the possibility that some of the plays performed in that time were directly critical of the King and his personal, non-parliamentary rule, but, as with the court masques we mentioned earlier, the messages of most plays remained decidedly equivocal on the subject. Their use of court-related forms, such as the masques, on the public stages, cannot, however, have failed to draw attention back to the space of the real court and its 'real-life' acts and actions.

The use of masques to resolve the action of a play was nothing new to Caroline dramatists. They were following a time-honoured theatrical tradition, inaugurated as early as the 1580s by Thomas Kyd's seminal revenge play *The Spanish Tragedy*, in which Hieronimo avenges the murder of his son in highly melodramatic fashion via a play performed in 'sundry languages' by both the perpetrators and the victims of that crime, and in which all are slain before an unwitting onstage audience's eyes. The idea of blurring fact and fiction in this way was taken up again by Shakespeare in his revenge tragedy *Hamlet, Prince of Denmark* (1601), where the young prince stages the 'Murder of Gonzago', a thinly veiled reference to his own father's murder, in order to test the guilt or innocence of his uncle Claudius, the new King:

> I'll have these players
> Play something like the murder of my father
> Before mine uncle.

> (Shakespeare, II. ii. 571–3)

In a witty displacement of Hamlet's death-scene (surely the ultimate scene for any male actor, the performance of which marks their achievement in the theatrical sphere), Massinger has Paris's fourth-act death and the carrying offstage of his corpse by grieving actors make a deliberately intertextual gesture to its Shakespearean predecessor. Other plays copied *The Spanish Tragedy*'s finale even more faithfully: John Webster has murderous masques and performances in *The Duchess of Malfi* and *The White Devil*, and Thomas Middleton has the same in *Women Beware Women* and *The Revenger's Tragedy*. James Shirley would re-employ their techniques in his own late Caroline tragedy *The Cardinal* (1640), in which the Cardinal's nephew, Columbo, murders his rival in love in the midst of a masque performance. The court, deception, and indeed violence were being inextricably linked in the audience's minds. The absolving explanation might always be that none of these plays were set in the English court (Webster's plays take place in a neo-Machiavellian Italy, as do Middleton's and Shirley's), but criticism of court behaviour must surely have been implicit.

John Ford also staged his courtly plays (*Perkin Warbeck* aside) in the worlds elsewhere of Italy, Cyprus, and Sparta, but once again his fondness for tropes and forms which were distinctly

Caroline in appearance, not least the masques and dances so favoured by Charles's court as a mode of self-presentation, would have meant that the 'real' court would not have entirely escaped implication in the midst of performances of the plays. Like Massinger, though, Ford is essentially respectful of the divinely sanctioned position of the ruler; it is rather the individual abuses of the role that he chastizes.

Ford has been credited by Ira Clark in his book *Professional Playwrights* as having a 'ceremonial style' and a 'restrained formality' (Clark, 85); certainly his work is deeply invested with the rituals and theatre of state. Climactic events in Ford often take place at traditional social gatherings – masques, dances, weddings, and banquets – and the nature of those traditions (and the institutions they represent) is tested by the events they contain. *The Broken Heart* in particular focuses on the rituals and ceremonies by which societies, in particular powerful societies, sustain and restrain themselves. Written in 1629 and first published in 1633, *The Broken Heart* is one of the period's most unrelenting, unremitting tragedies. There are no scenes of light relief to lift the tone, and the play processes forward at an almost stately, measured pace, mirroring in its entirety the remarkable final act in which the Princess Calantha (soon to be queen) maintains the ritual of the court dance even as she is informed in triple succession of the deaths of her father the King, her friend Penthea, and her lover Ithocles. This was exquisitely staged as a slow and perfectly choreographed dance of death in the 1994 Royal Shakespeare Company production of the play. Even Orgilus, who is sentenced to death for the murder of Ithocles, chooses to die a painfully visible onstage death, opening his own veins and watching the blood of life slowly draining from his body.

Such is Calantha's training in and dependence on these supporting court rituals that she is able to release her emotions and die only by means of the cathartic staging of her own 'mock-wedding'. The union can only ever be a grotesque parody because Ithocles is dead and Calantha weds an onstage corpse only for her heartstrings to break before our eyes, a quite literal reference to the play's title. Again, a painful parallel is effected, with the stage picture of the self-starved Penthea – Ithocles's twin sister – earlier in the play. Hers too was a broken heart, forced as she was into an unwanted marriage. The bringing onstage of her corpse in a chair (as if still alive) is a performance staged just like a masque, with its elaborate stage machines or 'engines'. This play-within-a-play's 'director' is Penthea's thwarted lover, Orgilus. He murders Ithocles because it was he who had prevented Penthea's marriage to the man she loved in favour of advancing his own court position by marrying his sister to the wealthy (and paranoically jealous) courtier Bassanes.

The Broken Heart is a play composed of stage tableaux, of dumbshow, masques, and music that contribute to an air of melancholy and fatalism that is all-pervasive. Tradition may be self-sustaining in terms of our social and communal identities; but, as Ford reveals in the individual tragedies of his drama, tradition and ritual can also be the very forms that constrain us, curb our free will, and crush our spirits. This is another stage littered with corpses: although Ford may well support the basic idea of monarchy, unthinking rule and adherence to rules is subjected to devastating critique in his drama.

As well as repeating and, to a large extent, revising traditional notions of the violence and deception of the court, *The Broken Heart* concerns itself with an issue of considerable interest and debate in the Caroline period: that of enforced marriage. The double standards of society are exposed in Ithocles's own cross-class attraction to Calantha and yet his refusal of a similar liaison between his sister and Orgilus; as Penthea tells him:

> Suppose you were contracted to her, would it not
> Split even your very soul to see her father
> Snatch her out of your arms against her will,
> And force her on the Prince of Argos?

> (Ford, III. ii. 106)

Orgilus, too, distraught at Penthea's condition (appalled at her marriage to a man she does not love, she chastizes herself as an adulterer and refuses to eat, descending into an Opheliaesque madness prior to her death), is not averse to controlling his own sister Euphrania's choice in marriage in an exchange that takes place at the start of the play. Patriarchy is under scrutiny in these playtexts, as are its sustaining rituals. The extent to which the discourses of the state and the family were connected in this period should not be underestimated. James I had regularly presented himself as the father of his subject-people, and it may be that criticism of domestic practice is a veiled means of criticizing patriarchal and paternalistic behaviour by the monarchy. Chapter 4 will explore these ideas further in the context of town-based comedies by Shirley and Brome.

All this should not, however, distract us from recognizing in Ford a very real recognition of the plight of women in his contemporary Caroline society, controlled as they were by the head males of the family in private and by patriarchy at large in the public sphere. Katherine Gordon, married off in *Perkin Warbeck* to the young pretender to the English crown at the King's behest, after her initial choice in love and partnership was rejected on class grounds by her father, is a further embodiment of this social subjection of women. Like Penthea, she never entertains the notion of rebellion, subjecting herself instead to loss of country and identity and eventually to the loss of her husband, executed as he is in the closing moments of the play.

John Ford's earlier 1630 play *'Tis Pity She's a Whore* is in many respects less a court play than a 'city tragedy', as the critic Verna Foster has so persuasively argued (Neill, 181–200). The action takes place in Parma, but in doing so it self-consciously exploits the associations of the Italian court with violence and Machiavellian scheming in much the same way as the Jacobean tragedies of Webster had done. Indeed, this play has a deeply intertextual relationship with a number of earlier tragic dramas set in Italy, such as *Romeo and Juliet*, *Othello* and *Women Beware Women*. We should also note that Parma was a city-state ruled over in the Italian Renaissance by the autocratic Farnese family, and so does provide important parallels with the English patriarchal court. James Shirley was to employ the same setting for his 1642 pastoral tragicomedy, *The Sisters*, which we will look at in Chapter 5. Italy was, then, a familiar tragic locale, providing the geographic and cultural impetus for Caroline tragedies, many of them modelled on earlier Elizabethan and Jacobean revenge tragedies, such as Ford's own *Love's Sacrifice* (1633), Brome's *The Queen and Concubine* (1636), and Shirley's *The Traitor* (1631) as well as *The Cardinal*.

In *'Tis Pity She's a Whore*'s Annabella, Ford creates another remarkable, if restricted, female protagonist. Unimpressed by her suitors, she realizes, not without cost to her conscience, that she is in love with her own brother, Giovanni. Their onstage vows provide an emotive stage moment:

ANNABELLA. Brother, even by our mother's dust, I charge you,
             Do not betray me to your mirth or hate;
             Love me, or kill me, brother.
GIOVANNI.   On my knees   (*kneels*)
             Sister, even by my mother's dust I charge you,
             Do not betray me to your mirth or hate;
             Love me or kill me, sister.

(I. ii. 244–9)

Their vows seem at first mirror images: they are twinned linguistically as they are biologically and sexually. But there is one crucial difference: Giovanni uses the possessive 'my' as opposed to Annabella's shared 'our'. The role of male possession and possessiveness in this play is already marked out for us as attentive audiences.

The actual patriarch of Giovanni and Annabella's family, Florio, is a benign one: he will not force his daughter to marry against her will and in this he differs radically from his precursor, Old Capulet in *Romeo and Juliet*, a play which is in so many ways invoked and inverted in Ford's story of a pair of star-crossed lovers: there is even an inverted balcony scene in which Annabella is, at that stage unwittingly, drawn erotically towards her brother in the shadows down below. It is rather Annabella's suitor, Soranzo – whom she is forced by circumstance to marry in order to hide the sinfulness of her sexual relations with her twin brother – and Giovanni himself, who prove a threat to her, both physically and emotionally. Their brutality and possessiveness is quite literally marked out on her body, by her broken hymen, her pregnancy, Soranzo's physical assaults, and Giovanni's ultimate decision to cut out her heart, thus killing both her and the unborn child. Patriarchal absolutism is still a pertinent theme in this play, although it may have been displaced from the figure of an actual monarch.

Court rituals in this play, as in *The Roman Actor* and *The Broken Heart*, are sites of corruption, death, and violence. In IV. i, at Annabella's wedding banquet, Giovanni's obsessive and self-destructive jealousy grows apace. Hippolita, to whom Soranzo was previously betrothed, participates in a masque with several other women by means of which she intends to poison her former lover. Vasques, whom she had assumed to be her supporter in revenge, thwarts her plan, however, and poisons her instead. The Friar (who is a touchstone for goodness in Parmese society and a conscious reworking of Romeo's father-figure Friar Laurence) reflects on the bad omen this represents for the marriage, and the audience is still aware of that prediction in Act V, when yet another doomed court feast is staged before its eyes.

The banquet of Act V is another of Ford's tragically disrupted communal gatherings, and can be likened to the perverted feast and the disturbed masque of *The Broken Heart*. Giovanni enters onto the court stage with Annabella's heart bleeding upon his dagger, and confesses his incestuous relations with his sister in public. Florio dies of grief, Giovanni murders Soranzo, and Vasques in turn kills Giovanni. In true tragic fashion, the stage is littered with corpses. The corruption of this autocratic society which had earlier enabled the shielding of the murderer Grimaldi from legal punishment is not resolved, however. Putana, Annabella's tragically disloyal servant, is now to be burned at the stake by the hypocritical Cardinal (who allowed the earlier cover-up), who will in turn gain from the tragedy by sequestering the goods and possessions of all those involved. Ford's point seems to be one to do with social status. Figures such as Giovanni and Annabella suffer not because of their sins but because of their lower social position. Giovanni at the beginning of the play is a bright but unsuccessful young man dependent upon others for his preferment in Parmese society – there are links between him and Ithocles in *The Broken Heart*, another twin brother who pawns his sister's emotions for self-promotion; Annabella, like Penthea, is besieged by suitors whom she must consider for her family's sake. Noble murderers in the meantime can escape arrest. Nothing is resolved by the end, and Caroline drama as a whole has been charged with failing to offer solutions to the social and political dilemmas it outlines (Clark). There seems to me, however, to be a radical honesty in Ford's drama, that may make its message hard to swallow but which should not be allowed to undermine its dramatic value.

Social inequity, then, is the subject most often under

examination in these court-based or court-related plays. That kings and princes live differently to their subjects was nothing new to observe, but the call for a more radical openness was (and is in part symbolized by the touching treatment of incest in *'Tis Pity She's a Whore*: Ford denies his audience the easy option of moral disgust). The redressing of social imbalances had its impact on gender as well as class relationships, and it is in theatre and the greater autonomy given to female protagonists in Caroline drama that I believe this can be most obviously registered. The irony of this is that this particular subversion of the patriarchal stranglehold came not from the lower or even urban sectors of society, but from within the court itself, and via the all-important masque form that we have been discussing here. Like those disrupted banquets and masques of Massinger's and Ford's tragedies, the subversion came from within and through that ultimate form of iconographic communal and cultural display – theatre itself.

3

Gender and Performance

This chapter will concern itself in part with the court theatricals of Charles I's wife, Queen Henrietta Maria. I want to move against the easy dismissal of the significance of these entertainments by a number of recent historians of the period, and to suggest for them a deep importance in the culture of the time – social, political, and religious – while arguing in addition for their strong influence on plays by the Caroline public-theatre dramatists under consideration here, in particular James Shirley and John Ford.

The historian Kevin Sharpe may suggest that Henrietta Maria only holds a backstage significance, at least in political terms, in the decade of the 1630s in his book *The Personal Rule of Charles I* (Sharpe, 173), but I want to stress the impact of her theatrical innovations at the Caroline court and to reinstate her 'playing', her commissioning of and performing in masques and entertainments throughout this period, at the centre stage of events.

In 1633, after all, William Prynne, the extremist writer of Puritan tracts and pamphlets inveighing against Papist threats to the nation, would have his ears removed in public by the public hangman for attacking court theatricals at length and in print, in particular the female theatricals of Henrietta Maria and her ladies-in-waiting. He did so in his 1,000-page tract *Histriomastix*, in which he famously equated women actresses with 'Notorious Whores' (the equation is evident in the index alone – Prynne was not afraid to nail his colours to the mast).

Play, plays, and playing were, then, highly political and politicized issues in the late 1620s and 1630s, and it is the nature and significance of that politicized play that I want to explore here by considering the court entertainments of Henrietta Maria and why they caused such moral and political controversy. In

30

doing so I want to argue that these spectacular events had a relevance and resonance far beyond the confines of the court; Prynne's text is itself firm evidence of this, but so too is the debate that raged about women and theatre on the public stages of the Caroline era. I want then to consider some of those plays engaged with questions of gender and performance from that time, in particular James Shirley's *The Bird in a Cage* (1633).

In the previous chapter we looked at Jacobean and Caroline court masques and their influence on plays for the public theatre, ostensibly tragic in genre, written by Ford and others. Court masques did become increasingly political in the early half of the seventeenth century – especially in the decade of the 1620s, when there were various European conflicts and complex diplomatic negotiations at the forefront of the English court's concerns. It is no coincidence that Henrietta Maria, who came to the throne with her husband in 1625 and who is closely associated with the Caroline masque, was a product of that European conflict – she was the daughter of the Queen Regent in France, Marie de Medici, and a product, therefore, of the troubled religious history of that nation.

Henrietta Maria, of course, was also a product of the French system of theatre and theatricals, and that too is significant. In the masques in which she performed at the Jacobean court in the early years of the 1600s Anne of Denmark had been, of necessity, silent. The silencing of women on the English stage extended from the court to the commercial theatres, where women's parts were played by boy actors. But Henrietta Maria was a product of a Continental tradition whereby women freely acted and spoke on both public and court stages. The introduction of Continental practices, to the court at least, with her arrival in England was to change English theatre forever. The professional theatres were closed down, and many of them were physically dismantled after 1642 with the outbreak of hostilities, partly for fear that they would function as sites of disorder. By the time of the reinauguration of London public theatre, which coincided with the restoration of the monarchy in 1660, theatre was restored in a transformed shape. In 1660 many royalist supporters returned from their self-imposed Continental exile where they had witnessed and frequently participated in theatre involving women performers and, as a

31

result, so accepted had the idea of women actors become by this time that the Restoration theatres opened with professional women actors and playwrights, such as Elizabeth Barry and Aphra Behn, installed at their heart.

Caroline masques have often been viewed as the most lavish of all the early modern court entertainments, a kind of fantasy world into which the troubled court escaped at regular intervals. But surface escapism should not tempt us into viewing these texts as apolitical. As with the politics of play and holiday in the Cavalier poetry of the decade by the likes of Herrick, Lovelace, Suckling, and Carew, the royalist trope of withdrawal may itself have deep political significance when placed alongside Puritan activism and prohibition against communal playing in the period. Masques were themselves closely allied to the festive or holiday calendar, performed as they were at Christmastime and Shrovetide, in that period of carnival free play just prior to Lenten abstinence, and about which Bakhtinian theory has been so eloquent and influential. We are dealing, then, with the politics of play and performance – sexual, theatrical, and political.

Henrietta Maria was French, protofeminist, and Catholic. She is credited with having introduced *preciosité* to the English court in the late 1620s: this was a movement, largely spearheaded by women, which involved the establishments of various *salons* in Renaissance France where like-minded people, men and women, would gather for conversation and the exchange of ideas. Those ideas were often protofeminist in their sympathies and, indeed, largely Catholic in their orientations. The *salons* espoused the doctrine of Platonic love and mutual non-sexualized respect and regard between the sexes, and venerated the virtues of love and beauty. The Catholic version of this manifested itself, of course, in veneration for the Virgin Mary. *Preciosité* and Marian and Platonic theories were flourishing in France when Henrietta Maria left for England and her marriage to Charles I in 1625.

It must be stressed that England in 1625 was deeply suspicious of Catholicism, and alarm bells must have rung over a spirited French Catholic queen who brought a number of French courtiers and, indeed, Capucin monks to accompany her to the English court. Henrietta Maria's Catholicism was in fact of a distinctly moderate nature – she was a so-called Devout Humanist, a school of Catholicism which was engaged in establishing a 'religion of love', most frequently associated with an interest in Neoplatonism and the cult of Platonic love that developed at this time (Veevers, 21–3).

The positive reading of Neoplatonism and related theories can be registered in a play such as John Ford's *Love's Sacrifice* (also published in 1633), the story of a love triangle in which the Duke of Pavia's new wife and his best friend, despite their genuine attraction to one another, contract to love platonically rather than go against the wedding vows. It should be said that, this being a tragedy, the woman at the centre of the triangle, Biancha, is killed by her jealous husband, who misunderstands the non-fleshly basis of the relationship between his wife and friend; but nevertheless the high-mindedness of Platonic love, as also gestured at in Jonson's *The New Inn* (a play we will consider in a moment) is evidenced. To Puritan spokespersons such as Prynne all of these developments were deeply disturbing. The themes of love and Platonic affection which the Queen favoured as subject-matter for her masques were read as being Papist in their intentions: Prynne feared that the Queen sought to convert the nation by seducing it through her feminine wiles and her erotic performances (*Histriomastix* is obsessed with the space of the bed and the Queen's bedchamber). Court plays were read as having covert religious and political messages within them by contemporaries, and we must attend to the contents as well as the spectacle of these masques and entertainments as a result.

Henrietta Maria had a particular penchant for pastoral. In 1626 she herself performed in a production of a Racine pastoral at the court, and this was read not only as a theatrical innovation (the Queen in a speaking role) but as an act of cultural intervention, introducing French ways to the English court. As well as breaching the taboo of royalty speaking onstage (there were fears of cultural taint and pollution: it was as though authority might be lost were a monarch to be seen to 'act' or dissemble in a part), Henrietta Maria went further, in having her fellow women actors play men's roles. These were consciously transgressive, consciously ground-breaking actions and performances. She went on to commission new works for her purpose, including Walter Montagu's eight-hour-long pastoral, *The Shepherd's Paradise*, which was performed in January 1633. It is thought that the rehearsals for this show and the gossip emanating from and around them stirred Prynne into print.

Of the nine masques presented at court between 1630 and 1640, four were the sole responsibility of the Queen, and it is possible to trace a specific set of images that related to her masques as opposed to Charles's and which, indeed, referred back to the Jacobean masques for Queen Anne (Veevers, 110). Such images are frequently Catholic in their significations, and it was no coincidence that Ben Jonson and Inigo Jones, chief creators of those earlier masques, had themselves been born Catholic, and that Anne was a crypto-Catholic (much to the concern of her subjects). Henrietta Maria's masques are highly Platonic in theme and tone: the associations are often with light and motion. The designs were the work of Jones, who at this time was also working on the designs for the Queen's House at Greenwich and, indeed, for her controversial construction of a Capucin chapel at Somerset House.

Her first masque, *Chloridia* (1631), is based on Ovidian myth, and in it the Queen played Chloris the nymph who transforms the earth to the beauties of Spring. It is the same story on which Botticelli's painting *Primavera* is based. *Tempe Restored*, performed in 1632, is also set in a garden (Henrietta Maria is often associated with nature and fertility, whilst her husband's masques are dominated by images of architecture and order – an obvious gendering of the iconography): the Queen played Divine Beauty, who banishes dangerous desire (in the shape of Circe) from the garden. In *The Temple of Love*, written by William Davenant in 1635, she took the role of Indamora, who re-establishes the Temple of Chaste Love in Britain. It was highly significant that the audience for the production was the Papal agent from the Vatican. At the time of the performance Inigo Jones was in the throes of the construction of the Capucin chapel at Somerset House, and these Catholic associations would have been inescapable and highly threatening to Puritan politicians and spokespeople. Not surprisingly, then, 1635–8 was a period of great optimism for Catholics in England, and a number of prominent courtiers openly converted to the faith (the very temptation Prynne had been so scared of in 1633) – Montagu, author of *The Shepherd's Paradise*, and Sir Kenelm Digby were amongst them. Openly celebrated masses were on the increase and, clearly, the Catholic sector of the population felt spurred on by the Queen's actions and support. The Archbishop of Canterbury grew anxious, however, and in 1637 reinforced laws against Catholics. But this proved to little avail when the Queen actively rebuked him by holding a Midnight Mass at her Chapel just five days later with many of those more famous recent converts to Catholicism present. It can be seen from all this, then, that Henrietta's statements in her theatre and in her religious life cannot be easily separated: they are all staged to the public eye and intended to be interpreted and 'read'.

The debate about women and theatre cannot and should not be extrapolated from a wider intervention on the Queen's part in the affairs of the country. The critic Sophie Tomlinson has suggested that female acting changed in status from a trope to a topic of discourse in the Caroline period (Tomlinson, 189–207): if it did then it was a discourse that overlapped with and intersected other discourses on religion and politics.

The engagement of public-theatre plays with that discourse and debate must therefore be viewed anew in this light. The Platonic themes of Ben Jonson's 1629 play *The New Inn* have often been noted, sometimes to suggest that he is attacking the Queen's tastes and the new feminocentric emphases at court. I am not convinced by this argument, and would suggest instead that the play is in some respects an agitation on behalf of female theatricals as well as being a deeply political playtext. It is again no coincidence that in 1629 Henrietta Maria had personally sponsored the performance of a French acting troupe, including speaking women actors, on the public stage at the Blackfriars theatre (the same stage on which the carnivalesque play of *The New Inn* was performed). The Queen was in fact a regular visitor to that theatre, often taking significant foreign dignitaries along with her, which is an indication of her valorization of the form.

Jonson examines the nature of illusions in general and of theatrical illusion in particular in *The New Inn*. A number of characters are playing assumed roles. The chambermaid Prudence assumes the guise of Queen for a day. When we first see Pru on stage, she and Lady Frances are troubled by the fact that the dress commissioned for the occasion has failed to arrive (causing a sadistic articulation of the proposed vengeance to be performed upon the tailor). Lady Frances Frampul's solution (and it is she who is often seen as a theatrical reworking of the Queen and her Platonic philosophies) is to lend Pru a dress of her own. Pru is considerably troubled by the social implications of dressing in her mistress's attire for such pranks. In this, she is not so far removed from 'anti-theatrical' contemporaries who questioned the morality of theatre, with its cross-dressed boys and its commoners attired as monarchs and nobles:

LADY FRANCES. 'Twill fit the players yet
            When thou hast done with it, and yield thee somewhat.
PRUDENCE.   That were illiberal, madam, and mere sordid
            In me, to let a suit of yours come there.
LADY FRANCES. Tut, all are players and but serve the scene, Pru:

                                        (Jonson, VI, II. i. 35–9)

It is significant that it is the aristocratic Lady Frances who is comfortable with the idea of theatre here: there is a sense in which theatre for women was as much determined by issues of rank and degree as gender. Henrietta Maria clearly did not regard it as illiberal to take her 'suits' to the Blackfriars theatre and to use that space to petition for her cause(s).

The performance of holiday is at stake in *The New Inn*, as indeed it was in the 1627 carnival play by a Suffolk schoolteacher called William Hawkins and entitled *Apollo Shriving*, in which the Prologue is spoken by a 'young scholar' who is in turn interrupted by a woman spectator demanding both a voice and a role in the play: 'Why should not women act men, as well as boys act women? I will wear the breeches, so I will.' The wearing of breeches would become a fact of the court theatricals of Henrietta Maria, of course, and is a concern as well as a focus for comedy in James Shirley's *The Bird in a Cage*. *The New Inn* involved cross-dressing by women (although at this stage female parts would still have been performed by boy actors), with Laetitia disguised as the boy Frank taking the part of Laetitia (that is to say, herself) in the course of the day's sports in the inn. Laetitia means 'joyfulness or gladness', and this was one of the virtues celebrated by Henrietta Maria's court circle: the inn itself is called 'The Light Heart', and all those associations of the Queen's masques with light and motion are conjured up here.

It is in this context, or these contexts, for Henrietta Maria's court plays that I want briefly to situate James Shirley's *The Bird in a Cage*, written, as I have said, in 1633 for the Cockpit theatre, of which the Queen herself was patron. Significant for my purposes is the fact that Shirley was recorded as being *valet de chambre* to Henrietta Maria at the time, and very much part of her feminocentric Catholic coterie at the court. Shirley was therefore involved in and sympathetic to female theatricals, and his text is ironic in its dedication to William Prynne, who at the time was in prison awaiting sentence (a 'bird in a cage' of a rather different kind to the one focused on by the play).

In brief, the plotline of the play is this: Eugenia, the Duke of Mantua's daughter, has fallen in love with Philenzo. Her father, however, refuses to accept the match, preferring to arrange a more lucrative husband for his daughter. To ensure Eugenia's obedience to his will in this matter he locks her up in a purpose-built tower along with her ladies-in-waiting. These women are forbidden any contact with men.

From this initial situation spring a number of plots devised by the male courtiers and the disguised Philenzo (now under the assumed name of Rolliardo – just to confuse matters further) to break into the tower. After various failures, he is successful when he hides in the central pillar of a cage of exotic birds presented as a gift to Eugenia, a tribute which makes obvious ironic reference to her incarcerated condition.

What is crucial to this play, however, is the means undertaken by the incarcerated women to pass the time. They decide to stage a play. All of the women, including the noble Eugenia, participate in the acting, and the 'play within the play' which they perform is the story of Jupiter and Danaë. This story, like that gift of caged birds, clearly refers to the women's situation, and is derived, like so many stories in early modern drama, from Ovid's *Metamorphoses*. Acrisius, Danaë's father, having been instructed by an oracle that a grandson will kill him, locks her in a brazen tower so that she cannot conceive a male child. Jupiter, however, visits in the form of a golden shower, resulting in the birth of Perseus (the image so exquisitely captured in art by Gustav Klimt in our own century and by Titian and Jan Gossaert, also known as Mabuse, amongst others, in the

Renaissance). In the women's play Eugenia, of course, plays Danaë. For all its theatrical subversiveness, with women playing men's parts and speaking their lines, this performance is conservative in its observance of social hierarchy for élite women. Like Henrietta Maria, Eugenia chooses a part which reflects her own social status as a nobleman's daughter as well as referring to her emotional and physical condition. One might recall that in her masques Henrietta Maria was never less than a princess in the parts she played. Eugenia acknowledges the relevance to her own story of the play's plotline:

DONELLA.   You like this story best then?
EUGENIA.   That of Jupiter and Danaë comes near our own.

(Shirley, II, IV. ii. pp. 429–30)

The performances of the women in service contain greater potential for transgression. Donella herself plays Jupiter, the ravishing god. Eugenia's ladies-in-waiting play the other parts, including the men's. As Donella puns in praising the skill of female performers: '[Shall] We! do not distrust your own performance. I have known men have been insufficient; but women can [always] play their parts' (III. iii. p. 416). There is much comment elsewhere in *The Bird in a Cage* on cross-dressing, with the men in female disguise attempting to enter the tower proving woefully inadequate in their performances. At the beginning of the third act Morello enters 'disguised like a lady', begging Jupiter for assistance with his petticoat (a phrase that gains added irony when Donella later plays the god's part in the women's playlet). As soon as he searches in his pockets for money with which to bribe the tower guards (a prosaic economic and reductive version of Jupiter's penetration of Danaë's tower in the form of a golden shower) he reveals his breeches and, in turn, his male inadequacies at performance in female disguise. The women's performance as men proves far more persuasive. The arrival of the gift of the caged birds interrupts the Jupiter–Danaë seduction scene, and Donella suggests what might have been, blurring the lines between 'acting' and truth quite self-consciously:

Beshrew the bell-man! an you had not wak'd as you did, madam, I should have forgot myself, and play'd Jupiter indeed with you; my imaginations were strong upon me, and you lay so sweetly.

(IV. ii. p. 435)

The subtext of rape is never far from the surface in Ovidian-inspired plotlines, and Philenzo/Rolliardo himself had earlier used the Jupiter–Danaë story as a facilitating myth for his own intent to fulfil the wager with the avaricious Duke of Mantua:

> I will fall upon her, as Jupiter on Danaë; let me have a shower of gold, Acrisius' brazen tower shall melt again; were there an army about it, I would compass her in a month, or die for it.
>
> (I. i. p. 381)

The lesbian implications of the theatrical exchange between Donella and Eugenia have been explored by critics (Traub). If we recall that on the stage the parts would in fact have been played by two boy actors there are also deliberately homoerotic implications as well, but Traub argues that the myth of Danaë and the trope of a play-within-a-play are a means of distancing audiences from any truly homoerotic possibilities or subversion in the women's performance. Yet it is worth noting how political attacks on the Queen were often expressed in erotic terms. Witness Prynne's bedchamber obsessions: the cultural stereotype of the woman-seducer, the idea of a 'second Eve', was at play here, but so too was the sexualization of her role which the Queen herself exploited in her court performances, dramatic or otherwise.

Margaret Cavendish, the Duchess of Newcastle and wife to William Cavendish, who actually collaborated with James Shirley in writing plays in the 1630s, was to rework this trope of a women's play in the 1660s for her own drama, *The Convent of Pleasure*, which features a female community governed over by the Lady Happy staging drama in exclusion from men (whilst those men try out various schemes to penetrate their space, including cross-dressing). It should be stressed that this female community is also invaded by men in disguise, in this instance the 'Princess', with whom Lady Happy finds herself falling in love (not without certain anxieties about her sexuality). What is fascinating about Cavendish's play, often described as a 'closet-drama', because written by a woman who was not a professional playwright and therefore never publicly staged, is that Cavendish when writing appears to have envisaged women players. The dynamics of performance and performative writing were definitely changing.

For James Shirley, of course, writing for the Caroline public stages, genuine women actors were not an option; but the decision he makes in *The Bird in a Cage* of juxtaposing successful female actors (actually boy-actors dressed as women dressed as men) with male characters manifestly failing in their female impersonations must have called to mind for contemporary audiences the equally successful performances of Henrietta Maria and her court women.

I am suggesting that it is possible to register a sea-change at this time in the approach to women and theatre. That sea-change can be traced as early as 1628–9 not only in Jonson's aforementioned *The New Inn* but also in John Ford's romance tragicomedy *The Lover's Melancholy*. In that play the female protagonist is the heroically named Eroclea. From the first moment that we see her onstage she is attired as a man and travelling under the assumed name of Parthenophill. We learn that she was destined to marry the Prince of Cyprus, Palador, but his father made violent sexual advances towards her, causing her to flee in the guise of a boy. With Agenor dead, she has returned to the court of the now melancholic prince, albeit in disguise. The end of the play will comprise of a Lear–Cordelia-esque reconciliation between Eroclea and her ailing father, now dressed in 'fresh raiments' like his Shakespearean tragic counterpart.

So persuasive is Eroclea's performance throughout that we see her aggressively wooed by not one but two women: Thamasta and her disloyal maid Kala. As if to further emphasize women's skill at performance, in the same play we have Grilla, a young woman disguised as a boy page (and reminiscent therefore of Viola's performance as Cesario in Shakespeare's *Twelfth Night*) and serving the foolish old man Cuculus who is indeed, in true Malvolio style, 'sick of self-love'. Not only does Grilla succeed in fooling the old man, but she is also enlisted to help in his amateur dramatic rehearsals for the 'Masque of Melancholy' which he intends to stage to the court. In the course of the rehearsals Grilla plays the roles of no less than three other women, all from different sectors of society, from maid to mistress, proving her acting skills and those of her sex beyond doubt: 'I know how to present a big lady in her own cue' (Ford, III. ii. 66–7). That Ford himself skilfully juxtaposes this metatheatrical scene with that where the persuasive actor Eroclea is pursued by her female admirers, and places both scenes at the centre of his play, suggests that women and acting, despite the inevitable appearance of boy actors in the roles of Grilla and Eroclea, was a central concern in designing this play.

Not all associations of women and theatre, and in particular women and masquing, were wholly positive or assertive. In Philip Massinger's *The City Madam* (1632), which I examine in more detail in Chapter 4, it is the determination of Lady Frugal and her self-willed daughters to perform their lives as if they were the Queen herself and her waiting women in court masques that exposes them to Luke Frugal's brutal humiliations: promising to deck them out as Juno, Iris, and other icons of female power familiar from the masquing tradition, he instead imprisons them in their home dressed in serving girls' aprons and prostitute's green. In James Shirley's 1642 play *The Sisters*, discussed further in Chapter 5, another vain and profligate woman, Paulina, conducts her country castle as if it were a court. This 'Semiramis' (another familiar female role from court masques), as she is termed by the forest bandits who set out to beguile her in the play, is a rather more pejorative account of female autonomy and performance than those representations I have been discussing here.

Shirley's plays were regularly performed at court to warm receptions, although the satire of his 1632 playtext *The Ball*, a comedy about London town life, was censored. In *The Ball* Shirley had one character, Jack Freshwater, arrogantly show off his knowledge of French societal and theatrical traditions by declaring, 'Women are the best actors, they play their own parts, a thing much desired in England by some ladies, inns o'court gentlemen and others' (Shirley, III, p. 79). There may be a covert reference here to William Prynne, who was himself an Inns of Court lawyer. Freshwater is undoubtedly assigned the buffoon's role in the play, and yet this should not blind us as spectators or readers to the seismic shift in female representations on the stage that was taking place in the 1620s and 1630s in the plays of Jonson, Ford, and Shirley amongst others. Gender and performance was a topic of high cultural currency. This may indeed be a reflection of French practice and, by extension, Caroline court practice at the time. If male impersonation of the female is as woefully inadequate as the cross-dressings of *The Bird in a Cage* by Morello and others prove to be, and the acting of Eugenia, Donella, and their companions as persuasive as the play of Danaë suggests, then demands for each sex to play their own were being articulated on the Caroline stage. By the Restoration these appeals had clearly been responded to as the first female actresses were being seen and heard on the English public stage.

4

City and Town

The idea of the city and the ever-burgeoning City of London spawned a great deal of literature and especially drama in the seventeenth century. Indeed, it spawned an entire genre in the Jacobean period: city comedy, as written and created by Ben Jonson, Thomas Middleton, and John Marston, amongst others. The *dramatis personae* of these city comedies invariably featured pickpockets, cozeners, and prostitutes, as well as the gullible members of the London gentry on whom such characters preyed. Famous examples would be Jonson's *The Alchemist* (1610) and *Bartholomew Fair* (1614), and Middleton's *A Mad World, My Masters* (1605) and *A Chaste Maid in Cheapside* (1611). The common locations of these plays were areas such as Southwark and Cheapside, many of which were to be found in the Liberties of London, the same place in which the commercial public theatres were constructed. These plays reflected London society back to their London theatre audiences and in turn influenced the London-based comic drama of the Restoration years after 1660. By the time of the drama of Congreve, Etheredge, and Wycherley, however, the locations depicted had undergone a geographic shift from the realm of the Liberties to the rather more well-to-do West End and the Strand. The focus was now on the world of the leisured classes rather than the economic districts Jonson had homed in on (although it should be added that Jonson had made his own forays into the domain of the leisured classes in the Strand in *Epicoene* (1609) which, not surprisingly, was a popular choice for revival in the Restoration theatres).

Philip Massinger's *The City Madam* (1632) is a play directly resonant of earlier Jacobean city comedies. Focusing on the fortunes and otherwise of the family of Sir John Frugal, including his profligate and dominating wife and daughters who clearly command all at home, the play is peopled by the usurers and down-at-heel aristocrats familiar from Middleton's plays and Massinger's own earlier *A New Way To Pay Old Debts*, explored in detail in Chapter 5. For this reason there is a tendency to read these plays as essentially nostalgic and backward-looking in their outlook and approach.

However, as I was stressing in the opening chapter to this book, it is important to redress the balance of theatre history, and to appreciate that the topographical shift in the Restoration theatre did not constitute a massive leap during the 1640s and the 1650s from Jacobean to Restoration sensibilities and social structures but had been in the process of social and theatrical transition during the Caroline period that preceded the decades of civil war and republican government. In the 1630s a large number of the plays of James Shirley and Richard Brome in particular employed city locations. In this respect they were engaging with the settings of the plays of their self-acknowledged Jacobean predecessors, most notably Jonson, who is so obviously alluded to in Brome's creation of Justice Cockbrain in *The Weeding of Covent Garden* (1632). Cockbrain declares himself to be following the precedent of *Bartholomew Fair*'s disguised Justice, Adam Overdo, who sets out to discover what he describes as 'the enormities of the fair':

> And so as my Reverend Ancestor Justice Adam Overdo, was wont to say 'In Heaven's name and the King's', and for the good of the Commonwealth, I will go about it.
>
> (Brome, II, I. i. p. 2)

Cockbrain intends the same for the Covent Garden locale, the significance of which we will consider later. But Shirley and Brome are also shifting the focus of their London comedies somewhat, in a manner that prefigures the town emphasis of Restoration comedy. Brome's decisive relocation from Jonson's Smithfield ('as dirty and as stinking every whit') to the more genteel and indeed centralized site of Covent Garden is paradigmatic of changing social relations in this respect.

London functions in all these plays as a microcosm of theatre itself. As a meeting-place and a catalyst for activity and no mere passive reflector of society, the capital city is depicted as being akin to the very theatre-houses in which it is being staged to the view. In this chapter I want to take several plays, one by Shirley, and three by Brome, as case studies for the significance of city and town spaces in the drama of the Caroline era: Shirley's *Hyde Park* (1632), and Brome's aforementioned *The Weeding of Covent Garden* (also known as *The Covent Garden Weeded*, and written and performed in the same year as *Hyde Park*), *The Sparagus Garden* (1635), and *The Antipodes* written in 1637.

Shirley's *Hyde Park*, as its title suggests, takes as its central location one of seventeenth-century London's largest open spaces. Indeed, the entire third and fourth acts of the play take place within the park's environs. Since Tudor times it had been the site of a royal game park, and was fenced in in order to protect the deer that roamed there. It was also far more distanced from the built-up areas of the city than it is today. Prior to the 1642–9 civil wars there were two keepers of the park. One of these in the Caroline years was Sir Henry Rich, who was appointed in 1612. In 1624 he became Earl of Holland, and it is to him that Shirley dedicates this play. Under Rich's control the park was opened to the general public for the first time. Shirley may be referring to this in his dedicatory epistle when he states that the first performance of *Hyde Park* was 'upon first opening of the Park', although it may just as easily suggest a spring date for the first performance, since the park opened according to the seasons.

In the Caroline 1630s Hyde Park was a meeting-place of considerable importance. Opened for the spring and summer months (something the play makes great use of in its references to spring and birdsong), it rapidly became a centre for sports and recreation, including the horse-racing which forms a plot element in Shirley's play (the races take place offstage and are proffered to us via vivid description, but the gambling attendant upon them has a significant onstage role). The park was also a site for potentially romantic or amorous encounters, and again the play's plotline, with its three love-chases, makes much of this creative and dramatic possibility.

It is to the park that Lacy and Mistress Bonavent go to celebrate their betrothal. Mistress Bonavent was formerly married to a merchant who has been missing at sea for seven years. She had promised her husband that she would wait that length of time before presuming him dead and considering remarriage. In truth, as we learn quite soon into the play (although Mistress Bonavent and the other characters remain unaware for a considerable time longer), Bonavent had been taken captive by a Turkish pirate, only recently securing his release. He returns to his own house in disguise, only to find his wife is to take a new husband that very day. Still in disguise, he goes with Lacy and his 'new wife' to the Park, eventually revealing his true identity to Mistress Bonavent whilst there, and later to the whole party. Lacy proves self-pitying but gracious in the face of this defeat: 'I was not ripe for such a blessing; take her, | And with an honest heart I wish you joys' (Shirley, II, V. ii. p. 540).

Also present in the park are the rakish Lord Bonvile – in some senses an obvious precursor of Restoration libertines such as Dorimant in Etheredge's *The Man of Mode* (1676) – Trier, and his beloved Julietta. The suspicious Trier, as his name suggests, has decided to test his lover by encouraging Bonvile's amorous attentions towards her, informing him that Julietta is a whore and therefore easy prey for his seductive wiles. Julietta, unaware of all these machinations, manages by means of her modest but assertive chastity to fend off Bonvile's approaches, refusing to believe ill of someone of his social standing. Ironically her act of faith forces Bonvile to control his behaviour and means that he fails to get her into bed despite his efforts throughout the play:

JULIETTA. I were too much wicked to suspect your honour,
         And in this place.
BONVILE. This place! The place were good enough,
         If you were bad enough, and as prepared
         As I. There have been stories, that some have
         Struck many deer within the Park.
JULIETTA. Foul play.
         If I did think your honour had a thought
         To venture at unlawful game, I should
         Have brought less confidence.

                                                      (IV. i. p. 508)

When Trier, with undisguised glee at his lover's moral rectitude, reveals his plot towards the end of the play, he informs Julietta:

         And I have found thee right
         And perfect gold, nor will I change thee for
         A crown imperial.

                                                      (V. ii. p. 536)

She, however, retorts almost immediately: 'And I have tried you, | And found you dross' (V. ii. p. 536). She rejects her jealous and suspicious partner as a prospective husband in favour of the chastened and tamed courtier, Bonvile. This neatly reverses the taming plot familiar from Shakespearean comedy, and looks forward to the achievements of Harriet over Dorimant in *The Man of Mode*. Martin Butler has gone so far as to suggest that Julietta's triumph is that of her class: of solid gentry values over the false ones of the court. Although this may be too radical a reading, there is no doubt that Shirley's inversion of several romantic truisms in his drama deserves comment.

The third love-chase, on which emotion as well as wealth is gambled in the course of the play, involves three male suitors – Fairfield, Venture, and Rider. All are vying for the attentions of the seemingly disinterested Mistress Carol. Carol is another of Shirley's independent female voices. She chides her friend Mistress Bonavent for so readily surrendering the freedoms and liberties (as she perceives them) of widowhood and status for Lacy's offer of marriage, telling her:

> You are sick of plenty and command; you have
> Too, too much liberty, too many servants;
> Your jewels are your own, and you would see
> How they will shew upon your husband's wagtail.

> (I. ii. p. 475)

Carol is termed a tyrant by more than one character for her rejection of male attentions. She advises Mistress Bonavent to:

> Imitate me; a hundred suitors cannot
> Be half the trouble of one husband. I
> Dispose my frowns and favours like a princess;
> Deject, advance, undo, create again;
> It keeps the subjects in obedience,
> And teaches 'em to look at me with distance.

> (I. ii. p. 475)

There is much play here and elsewhere throughout *Hyde Park* on women's sovereignty in love: it is the men in this play who are reduced to the social status of subjects and servants. Carol takes jewels from one suitor only to give them to another in a very obvious rejection of their value, gulling each man in turn. Her behaviour is forced to undergo a shift, however, when Fairfield (clearly wounded by her disinterest) forces her to promise never to love him. By forbidding the very feelings for him that he so desires, Fairfield (Julietta's brother) frees the wilful Carol to realize her genuine affections: she reflects:

> I must confess you have caught me; had you still
> Pursued the common path, I had fled from you;
> You found the constitution of women
> In me, whose will, not reason, is their law;
> Most apt to do, what most they are forbidden,
> Impatient of curbs in their desires.

(III. ii. p. 504)

She feels bound, however, by her sworn oath, publicly continuing to deride him, in one wonderful instance making a witty inversion of the traditional poetic blazon of the female face:

> Would I had art enough to draw your picture,
> It would show rarely at the Exchange; you have
> A medley in your face of many nations:
> Your nose is Roman, which your next debauchment
> At tavern, with the help of pot or candlestick,
> May turn to Indian, flat; your lip is Austrian,
> And you do well to bite it; for your chin,
> It does incline to the Bavarian poke,
> But seven years may disguise it with a beard,
> And make it – more ill-favoured; you have eyes
> Especially when you goggle thus, not much
> Unlike a Jew's; and yet some men might take 'em
> For Turk's, by the two half moons that rise about 'em –
> [*Aside*] I am an infidel to use him thus.

(III. ii. pp. 505–6)

In an aside Fairfield laments: 'I have made twigs to jerk myself' (III. ii. p. 504).

Later however, falsely believing a suicidal note to be from Fairfield, Carol offers to marry him out of kindness. Initially he spurns this offer, but this in turn forces her into a public declaration of her true affections for him, and the sparring lovers are eventually contracted to be married. This bantering duo has dramatic forerunners of its own in Petruchio and Kate in *The Taming of the Shrew*, in Rosaline and Biron in *Love's Labour's Lost* and most obviously in Beatrice and Benedick, those self-knowing lovers of *Much Ado About Nothing*, whose 'merry war' endures for much of that play.

48

Like Shakespeare's Benedick, Shirley's Fairfield has clearly met his marital and linguistic match: Carol declares that even if married she will not:

> ...be confined to make me ready
> At ten, and pray till dinner; I will play
> At gleek as I please, and see
> Plays when I have a mind to't, and the races...

> (II. iv. p. 490)

Marriage was a social institution undergoing transition at this time. Arranged marriages were still the norm amongst the propertied classes, especially those with daughters, who were regularly married off for economic and dynastic ends. Brides, however, were increasingly being allowed greater say in the choice of a husband, particularly in rejecting those they deemed unsuitable for a lifetime's partnership. This right of choice is asserted by all the women in *Hyde Park*, and the double standards of a society that persecuted women for adultery but allowed men mistresses is also exposed at various turns. It has been suggested that the penchant at court for depicting the marriage of Charles I and Henrietta Maria as a romantic as well as political one (she was, after all, the French monarch's sister) influenced a new approach to the nuptial contract in the social mainstream. What is clear from the assertions of female and male characters alike in this play is that women were demanding a greater say in the determination of their fates: for example, Carol rejects Mistress Bonavent as a role model in her willingness to wed:

> Oh love, into what foolish labyrinths
> Dost thou lead us! I would all women were
> But of my mind, we would have a new world
> Quickly.

> (I. ii. p. 470)

This 'new world' of female performance and assertion we have traced elsewhere in the masques and masque-influenced drama of the Caroline era. Equally vocal female characters can be found in Jonson's *The New Inn* and *The Sad Shepherd*, and in other plays by Ford, Brome, and Shirley. When Angellina questions, in the course of Shirley's *The Sisters*, whether women wear spurs, the answer is returned that they may do in time. As Fairfield reflects in *Hyde Park*: 'This is a new doctrine, | From women' (I. ii. p. 472).

It is around the institution of marriage, formerly prescribed by patriarchy, that this new doctrine is most obviously realized on the Caroline stage. Parents are very noticeably absent from the youthful population of *Hyde Park*. Children more manifestly reject parental instruction in the choice of partners in a number of the other town-based plays by these dramatists, not least Richard Brome's *The Weeding of Covent Garden*, which interweaves no less than three plots of children going against their parents' wishes in choosing marriage for reasons of affection rather than status or wealth. We have the children of Rooksbill the architect, Justice Cockbrain, and the eternally furious Crosswill, all seeking to find freedom through marriage and their choice of marital companion.

Crosswill in particular is the embodiment of overweening patriarchal authority. For him authority is power, and even when his children prove obedient (as in Katherine's bending to his will over her marital prospects) he suspects them of challenging his right to impose his arbitrary power upon them:

> La there again! How subtly she seeks dominion over me! No, huswife, No; you keep no house of mine. I'll nestle you no longer under my wing. Are you not fledge; I'll have you fly out I, as other mens daughters do; and keep a house of your own if you can find it.
>
> (Brome, II, I. i. p. 7)

Of course, Katherine, like her brother Mihil, finds means of achieving liberty from the dominant patriarch via seeming compliance, and this may in turn cast an interesting light on the wider politics of the 1630s. It was a decade of non-parliamentary rule, in which the king's arbitrary introduction of new laws and national taxation came in for some criticism. Since the King regularly depicted himself as the father of the nation, it is just possible that this critique of family relations and in particular of overweening patriarchs in the plays of Brome and others might be a coded reference to the monarchy.

In emphasizing the town locale of many London-based Caroline plays, it is important to register royal opposition to the town and all it represented, not least Covent Garden, the centre of gentry foothold in the city. As Martin Butler has described in *Theatre and Crisis*, the square was quite deliberately designed as fashionable housing for the gentry sector of society. Even in this, Covent Garden was controversial. There was a royal proclamation at the time against the construction of new buildings in London. Covent Garden was in fact made possible only through the efforts and influence of its architect, Inigo Jones. He was the commissioner for new buildings and could authorize rebuilding on old foundations, provided it was done with 'Uniformity and Decency'. This was the case he made for Covent Garden. Cockbrain certainly seems impressed in the opening scenes of Brome's play, telling Rooksbill (clearly a stage version of Jones):

> I Marry Sir! This is something like! These appear like Buildings! Here's Architecture expressed indeed! It is a most sightly situation, and fit for Gentry and Nobility.

> (I. i. p. 1)

This is clearly a spirited defence of Covent Garden against royalist objections. In this there could also be seen a political analogue. Crown opposition to the project is rejected on the grounds of the 'decency' and precedent of the project:

> It will be glorious: and yond magnificent Piece, the *Piazzo*, will excel that at Venice, by hearsay, (I never travelled). A hearty blessing on their brains, honours, and wealths, that are Projectors, Furtherers, and Performers of such great works.

> (I. i. p. 1)

Parliament in the 1640s justified many of its projections and criticisms of the crown on the grounds of ancient precedent. The geographical setting of *The Weeding of Covent Garden* places the play in a critical and potentially subversive position in relation to the crown.

The Earl of Bedford was the chief property developer in the area and he, like a number of the dedicatees of Brome's drama, was an aristocrat who often found himself in conflict with the crown (he had been a champion of the Petition of Right in 1629, and spent six months in prison for his involvement in the events which led to the closure of Sir Robert Cotton's library). Covent Garden, and by implication Bedford, also placed itself in opposition to Charles's Archbishop of Canterbury, William

Laud, by constructing the first new church in England since the Reformation. Here was a new doctrine indeed. But his setting of the play in this subordinate locale is not the sole indicator of Brome's investment in a critique of the Caroline monarchy and, by implication, the Personal Rule. The play is 'larded with allusions to the intensified royal paternalism of 1632–4' (Butler, 148). There are references to royal proclamations on prices, the *Book of Sports*, the licensing of the taverns, and the creation of the controversial soap monopoly; but most significantly, it seems to me that Brome uses the three parallel relationships between fathers and children as a means of questioning Charles's arbitrary form of government at the time.

Restrictive paternalism is also a theme in Brome's 1635 *The Sparagus Garden*, another play that takes place in the potentially oppositional space of the town. Its title is based on the rather wonderful premise that asparagus is a new exotic variety of vegetable that has just been introduced into the country, and such is the desire to taste it that a hotel has been established solely for the purpose. All kinds of powers, not least aphrodisiac, are ascribed to the plant in question, but of course in practice the hotel becomes little more than a high-class brothel, the consumption of the wonderfully phallic asparagus spears becoming a convenient euphemism for sexual dalliance and promiscuity. Here we have another model of subject children's resistance to dubious parental authority (although once more this rebellion is performed only reluctantly, and not for rebellion's sake – again, an interesting take on subsequent parliamentarian attacks on 'the father of the country').

Two older men, Touchwood and Striker, ironically both Justices of the Peace – clearly a favourite target for Brome's satire, as they had been for his former master Jonson – are engaged in a bitter legal dispute (Brome's plays frequently attack legal gains from private disputes: the one in this particular play prefigures the endless 'Jarndyce versus Jarndyce' legal trial of Charles Dickens's nineteenth-century novel *Bleak House*). The dispute was prompted by something so trivial no-one can remember what it was, but it has endured nine years, consuming their families along with their family wealth. Touchwood, it seems, has cast off his own son due to the affections he has developed for Striker's daughter.

In the second scene of the play we see Sam Touchwood, the son, deliberating over the advisability of going against patriarchal authority:

> To disobey a father is a crime
> In any son unpardonable. Is this rule
> So general that it can bear no exception?
> Or is a father's power so illimitable
> As to command his son's affections?

(I. ii. p. 121)

The resonance of this for a society debating the pros and cons of challenging the royal prerogative is surely inescapable: like a sovereign, patriarchy 'commands'. Encoded within the domestic locale, Brome's play draws attention to the topicality of its subject matter through the choice of vocabulary.

Interestingly, the role of father or patriarch is somewhat unstable in its interpretation in this play; Annabell, the object of Sam's affections, turns out to be Striker's granddaughter: paternity has then become a blurred or questionable subject. Like many of Brome's plays, there is scarcely a conventional plotline, rather a series of juxtaposed episodes which all involve rebellion against paternalism in some form or other. The central conceit of the asparagus garden, once used, is never returned to, but like the tavern roistering of the 'brotherhood' in the central act of *The Weeding of Covent Garden*, it serves to show a society in crisis, its natural forms under pressure and in transition.

In the last play I want to look at in detail here, Brome's 1637 drama *The Antipodes*, London is actually given a fictional counterpart, Anti-London, supposedly the capital city of the Antipodean nation of the title. In truth, the 'journey' to the Antipodes undertaken by the protagonist Peregrine is entirely fictional. This disturbed youth is so anxious to travel to the lands he has read about in the travel books of Sir John Mandeville and others (and Brome and his audiences would have been well aware of the ironic truth that Mandeville's own texts were carefully woven fabrications) that he has rejected his wife Martha and descended into a kind of clinical depression – described in the play as 'Mandeville madness'. He is persuaded by Dr Hughball and the theatrical figure of Lord Letoy that he has swallowed a potion and travelled to the other side of the world. What this dramatic representation of a carnivalesque 'world-turned-upside-down' on the public stage enables Brome to do is to safely satirize contemporary London by displaying a place that is, as is constantly stressed, tantamountly *not* London. At times Anti-London, where men are subjected to the ducking stool as scolds, where lawyers are honest, and where women are seen on top, sexually and in the domestic arena of the household, is intended as the direct antithesis of Caroline London, highlighting the inequalities of the real society of the watching audience (onstage and off) by depicting alternative modes of living: at others, though, the relationship is one of proximity rather than distance. The Antipodean city-state frequently performs the function of a mirror, critiquing some of the social realities of contemporary 1630s Caroline society simply by reflecting them back to its inhabitants. Doctor Hughball may claim:

> This, sir, is Anti-London. That's the antipodes
> To the grand city of our nation:
> Just the same people, language, and religion,
> But contrary in manners, as I ha' told you.
>
> (Brome, III, II. iv. p. 264; *Antipodes* II. iv. 38-41)

but we come to see that the behaviour of the Antipodean natives is not so far removed from that of the London inhabitants we have been witnessing onstage thus far.

Once again Martin Butler has traced potentially subversive political commentary within this play in his *Theatre and Crisis*. The world turned upside down, he argues, is being proffered as a form of dramatic counsel to the monarch. When the play was first performed Charles I had been governing for almost a decade without summoning a parliament. Brome, Butler suggests, is offering the advice that Charles should turn his autocratic style of government 'upside down', and by implication summon a parliament and listen to those subjects who were opposing unparliamentary innovations in the period, such as Ship Money, raised, as its name suggests, to maintain the navy, and other extraordinary taxations which had been levied on the population. In the parodies of the legal world contained within the play staged at Letoy's house in the course of *The Antipodes*, Butler identifies allusions to specific cases such as the drawn-out hearings over Ship Money in the late 1630s. The play is seen to hit home despite its mode of high fantasy.

All of this is 'staged' both to Peregrine and his companion onstage audience, and to the audiences of the Salisbury Court theatre where *The Antipodes* was first performed, by means of the familiar early-modern metatheatrical technique of a play within a play. Brome, like Massinger in *The Roman Actor* and, indeed, *The City Madam*, where the fifth-act 'Masque of Orpheus' reforms the wicked actions of the power- and wealth-crazed Luke Frugal, and Ford in *The Lover's Melancholy*, appears to lay faith in the curative and transformative power of theatre. The voyage into fantasy is not over until the audience decides it is with their applause:

> And from our travels in th'Antipodes
> We are not yet arrived from off the seas;
> But on the waves of desperate fears we roam
> Until your gentler hands do waft us home.
>
> (V. xi. p. 339; *Antipodes* V. xii. 40–44)

The last word of this play is 'home'. The fantasy of travel is, in the end, a means of reinterpreting one's own place and space. Brome's play is exploiting the theatrical nature of the city-space itself: theatre, as in *Hyde Park* and *The Weeding of Covent Garden*, provides a meeting-place akin to that provided by the city itself, a site for exploration, education, and self-investigation. Both *The Antipodes* and *Hyde Park* go one stage further in this respect, creating an alternative space within London for such self-fashionings to occur. The significance of Peregrine's fantasy of world travel has already been discussed; the Hyde Park location of Shirley's eponymous play offers a space equivalent to Shakespeare's magical and metaphorically loaded Forest of Arden in *As You Like It*: a 'green world' in the midst of urban reality. It is, as Martin Butler has stressed, a meeting-place for town and country, art and nature. As the Caroline reign progressed, the countryside became a crucial site for opposition to the autocratic government of the period of Personal Rule. In the final chapter of this book, I therefore want to move outside of the city altogether and into the realm of plays where the crucial site is the country, and to consider the significance, dramatic and socio-political, of the communities depicted there.

5

Country and Community

If Caroline dramatists demonstrated an immense and creative interest in urban locales and tropes of the city for their plays, so too did they find in the English countryside a setting ripe for dramatic appropriation. The deployment of non-urban locations, of regions that were far more clearly 'not-London' than Brome's Anti-London dream-world in *The Antipodes*, was not, however, a fixed or static strategy throughout the period. This chapter will chart the intrinsic shifts and transitions in understandings of the countryside and their manifestation on the Caroline public stages, beginning with one of the earliest Caroline dramas, Philip Massinger's *A New Way to Pay Old Debts* (composed in 1625, the year of Charles's accession, although not published until 1633), and ending with two plays at the other end of the chronological spectrum which were, to all intents and purposes, the last publicly staged dramas in England before the civil war: Richard Brome's *A Jovial Crew* (1641) and James Shirley's *The Sisters* (1642). Tropes of the country will be seen to shade into debates about community that were to prove central to the political and social upheavals of the Caroline period and beyond.

A New Way to Pay Old Debts is a play that is still, regularly, if not frequently, revived on the stage. Part of the reason for its enduring popularity in the theatre is undoubtedly Massinger's central and vibrant creation of his villainous protagonist, Sir Giles Overreach, a positive gift for any comic actor to perform. Sir Giles, as his name suggests, is a post-Marlovian overreacher, a social aspirant to wealth, title, and influence who is prepared to stop at nothing to achieve his ends. In *A New Way to Pay Old Debts* we see him mercilessly engineer the marriage of his reluctant daughter Margaret to an ageing aristocrat: 'She must part with | That humble title, and write honourable, | Right honourable' (II. i. 74–6); preparing the enclosure of his neighbour's lands: 'I'll make my men break ope his fences, | Ride o'er his standing corn, and in the night | Set fire on his barns, or break his cattle's legs' (II. i. 35–8); and both encouraging the downfall of his profligate aristocrat-nephew Wellborn, whose lands he has sequestered, and then, when he wrongly assumes Wellborn's fortunes are about to rise again by means of marriage to the aristocratic widow Lady Allworth, paying off the prodigal's considerable debts. Without conscience, Overreach informs his nephew that his change of heart is entirely justified:

> We worldly men, when we see friends, and kinsmen,
> Past hope sunk in their fortunes, lend no hand
> To lift 'em up, but rather get our feet
> Upon their heads, to press 'em to the bottom
>
> (III. iii. 503–6)

All this is interspersed with displays of cruelty and violence towards his servants and members of his own family unequalled on the early modern comic stage. Little surprise is it then that when his conscience finally breaks his sanity, the gargantuan figure of Overreach feels himself literally weighed down by the memory of those he has ruined:

> Some undone widow sits upon mine arm,
> And takes away the use of't; and my sword,
> Glu'd to my scabbard with wrong'd orphans' tears,
> Will not be drawn.
>
> (V. i. 362–5)

Overreach is rightly viewed by critics as a theatrical creation which evidences its own debts to the monomaniacs of Ben Jonson's satiric comedies: figures such as Volpone in the eponymous 1606 play (who, like Overreach, finds himself ensnared in his own traps), Sir Epicure Mammon in *The Alchemist* (1610), who himself lusts after wealth and power in the extreme, and Fabian Fitzdottrel in *The Devil is an Ass* (1616), who uses his wife Frances as a commodity for sale much as Overreach does his daughter, and who also finds his lands and money lost by the end of the play. For this reason it has been suggested that Massinger is seeking to criticize the new middle classes of urban London, who were buying their titles and their way into power, in the same way as Jonson's treatment of social aspirants and arrivistes has been read from the time of L. C. Knights's criticism onwards (Smith, 183–92). I have my reservations about these theoretically one-dimensional readings of Jonson; despite the overtly moralistic tone of the fifth act in *A New Way to Pay Old Debts* (with Wellborn's speech of redemption placed in juxtaposition to Overreach's very public descent into madness), I would suggest that similar ambiguities and tensions exist in Massinger's own depictions of his contemporary society, not least in the highly nostalgic, but largely passive, behaviour of his ageing aristocrats, Lord Lovell and Lady Allworth. The latter pair's solemn contract of marriage at the end of the play may provide a happy ending in true comic tradition, but their age and position in life suggests a neat closure of a former way of living, a rounding-off rather than a movement towards pastures new.

In many respects this play *is* self-consciously backward-looking. In the opening scene we have the innkeeper Tapwell's narrative of Wellborn's former greatness and his valorization of Wellborn's late father:

> I'll briefly tell your story. Your dead father,
> My quondam master, was a man of worship,
> Old Sir John Wellborn, Justice of the Peace, and Quorum,
> And stood fair to be *Custos Rotulorum*;
> Bore the whole sway of the shire; kept a great house;
> Reliev'd the poor, and so forth; but he dying,
> And the twelve hundred a year coming to you,
> Late Master Francis, but now forlorn Wellborn...
> You were then a lord of acres, the prime gallant,
> And I your under-butler; note the change now.
> You had a merry time of't. Hawks, and hounds,
> With choice of running horses; mistresses
> Of all sorts, and all sizes, yet so hot
> As their embraces made your lordships melt;

> (I. i. 32–9; 42–7)

As this telling indicates, Wellborn's life-text has much in common with the prodigal-son figures and debased aristocrats of the Jacobean city comedies of Middleton, in particular *A Trick to Catch the Old One* (1605); but it is worth noting that the prodigal-son model was a popular one in the drama produced in the early years of the Caroline reign – Jonson's 1626 play *The Staple of News* opens on the stage with the visible profligacy of its central protagonist Pennyboy Junior as he spends away the inheritance he is only just about to achieve with the clock's striking of midnight and his move into legal adulthood. Intriguingly, this play has other links with Massinger's production of just a year earlier in its central cook-figure Lickfinger, clearly a larger reworking of *A New Way to Pay Old Debts*'s Furnace. Perhaps the débâcle of the doomed 'Spanish Match' in 1623, when Charles I, then Prince of Wales, had failed in his attempt to marry the Spanish Infanta was now being publicly forgiven as he ascended the throne. The king himself might be seen as the prodigal come home.

Even though it looks back to earlier theatrical traditions, not least the morality plays and city comedies, and indeed Shakespearean comedy in its intricate revisions of the domestic household of the mourning Olivia which was created on the stage of *Twelfth Night* – in *A New Way to Pay Old Debts* we have a steward, Order, a mourning mistress who refuses the carnival-esque spirit of her kitchen, and a challenge to social hospitality and festivity in the form of Lady Allworth's household – Massinger's play is nevertheless a product of its own cultural moment. Even the theatrical *tour de force* that is Sir Giles had basis in a real-life scandal over monopolies that had plagued the latter parliaments of James I's reign, and which in 1621 had seen the impeachment of the nobleman held responsible for gross abuses of crown prerogatives, Sir Giles Mompesson.

Massinger's play can fruitfully be read, then, as a Caroline social document. It was also a play that had a considerable effect on the kind of drama produced afterwards. Not only did Jonson's *The Staple of News* echo the prodigal-son plotline, but his 1629 play *The New Inn* (which, like *A New Way to Pay Old Debts*, signals its new take on old traditions in its title) takes place in an inn outside London, an intertextual gesture towards that opening scene in Tapwell's Nottinghamshire alehouse in Massinger's play. As one of its central roles it also has the ageing and nostalgic aristocrat (and significantly named) Lord Lovel, whose conscious articulations of the lost values of contemporary society echo the exchanges between Lovell and Lady Allworth in the fourth act of *A New Way to Pay Old Debts*.

In describing Wellborn's late father, Tapwell is careful to emphasize his significant role as a local magistrate, a Justice of the Peace, indeed, one who was set to become the recordkeeper of the shire Quarter Sessions (*Custos Rotulorum*). Tapwell himself, having refashioned his career as an innkeeper after the demise of the Wellborn estate (where he was formerly under-butler), is proud of his own participation in local office, currently as Scavenger (someone charged with keeping the streets clear of rubbish), but has social aspirations to reach the dizzy heights of being Overseer of the Poor (charged with the administration of poor relief). This is the world of petty local officialdom and regional issues that was to be so fruitfully explored in Jonson's 1633 play *A Tale of a Tub* (written the same year that *A New Way to Pay Old Debts* was published). That play, which also features a noble family fallen into immoral ways after the death of its exemplary patriarch, focuses on the neighbourhood watch and the disastrous attempts of the local high constable, Toby Turf, to marry off his daughter Audrey on a freezing cold St Valentine's Day.

This new focus in the drama of the late 1620s and the 1630s on the shires and the world outside London has definite implications for the Caroline government of the time. In 1629, and in a course of events to which Jonson's *The New Inn* makes extended reference, Charles I, in refusing to accept the Petition of Right put forward by his ministers, dissolved parliament. He did not summon another until the Short Parliament of 1640. This period of non-parliamentary rule has come to be known by various names – the Personal Rule, the King's Peace, and the Eleven Year Tyranny – depending on the viewpoint of the historical commentator. What is important for our purposes here is to note that with the extended pause in the summonings of parliament, increasing amounts of bureaucratic pressure and responsibility were pushed back onto the provinces, and these 'country' locations grew in their importance to the centre and indeed in their ability to influence Crown affairs; not least in the area of tax collection, which in the widespread failure or refusal in 1637 to pay Ship Money (an extraordinary form of taxation levied by Charles without parliament's permission in the 1630s to raise money for his stretched Treasury coffers) contributed directly to the events that led to the outbreak of hostilities between parliament and the King in 1642.

It is this changed and newly politicized countryside locale that forms such a rich focus for dramatic events in Richard Brome's *A Jovial Crew*. Briefly, the plot of this busy and energetic play is that by the time the drama commences, a benign aristocratic estate-owner, Oldrents, has been told by a gypsy fortune-teller that there are dangers ahead for his two daughters, Rachel and Meriel. So struck down with anxiety is Oldrents as a result that his previously jovial and hospitable household becomes a site for melancholy and confinement, much to his daughters' distress. Rachel and Meriel therefore decide to run away from their father, and their two gentleman companions, Vincent and Hilliard, agree to accompany them. They find the means for their escape in the shape of the household steward, Springlove, who has found his own reasons to leave. In the opening act we see Springlove declare to his master that he must answer the calls of spring and the countryside (signified on stage by the sound of the nightingale's song) and leave his steward's post until winter time, joining the crew of beggars currently being given shelter in Oldrents's barn on their countryside wanderings. Rachel, Meriel, Vincent, and Hilliard decide to become beggars themselves, dressing in rags and living off the hedgerows and briars of the world beyond Oldrents's considerable estate.

Much of the play focuses on the experiences of these aristocrats in disguise. Unsurprisingly they find their romantic views of the 'beggars' commonwealth', as it is so frequently referred to by the play, tested by the reality of hunger, cold, and sleepless nights. Eventually arrested, along with the rest of the 'jovial crew' of beggars, by Justice Clack and his neighbourhood watch team, they are nevertheless given the opportunity to perform a play before their own father. If it pleases his countenance (now surprisingly merry since the focus of his anxieties – his daughters – has gone away) they are to be excused the stripping and whipping Clack is so anxious to mete out to them. The play they perform, the story of *The Merry Beggars*, is in many respects Brome's play in microcosm. In true comic tradition, the play proves a success and the estranged family is reconciled.

There are some significant sub-plots to the play, in particular the story of Amie who has escaped her uncle Clack's arranged marriage for her to the foolish and inane Tallboys by running away to the countryside with the household clerk, Martin. Stumbling upon the begging community, Amie finds herself falling in love with Springlove and eventually marrying him in a hedgerow ceremony. The jealous Martin escapes back to Clack and informs on the whereabouts of Amie and the beggars, leading to the pursuit and arrest of the community. By the end of the play proper, however, both Martin and Tallboys have lost Amie to Springlove and, indeed, the oppositions to Amie's marriage on class grounds have been removed by the Patrico or hedge-priest's revelation that Springlove (who was a beggar before Oldrents rescued him from that life, installing him as a servant in his own household) is in reality the son of the Patrico's late sister and Oldrents himself, and therefore heir to the estate. This, it seems, was the threat to Rachel and Meriel's inheritance that Patrico had foretold to Oldrents before the play began, and in the context of the drama it proves to be an entirely fortuitous one in that Rachel and Meriel find a brother in Springlove who has throughout been a good guardian to them.

Brome's play, then, both invokes and subverts the familiar genre of dramatic pastoral, a form which had undergone a revival of sorts in the Caroline period, in particular in the context of Henrietta Maria's whimsical court commissions. In putting his courtly characters, such as Vincent and Hilliard, through a testing of the pastoral ideal Brome continues a rather more sceptical interpretation of the form that had been an integral part of Shakespeare's own invocation and pressurizing of the genre in *As You Like It* in 1599.

Vincent and Hilliard admire what they see as the unproblematic felicity and happiness of the beggars' community: 'They are the only people can boast the benefit of a free state' (Brome, III, II. i. p. 370; *Crew*, II. i. 2–3). Their comments suggest that the life of aristocrats is one of care and responsibility which the countryside dwellers are free of. The naivety this view demonstrates will of course be sorely tested by the realities of a life of living in barns and off their wits: by the time we see them onstage in their beggars' rags, Vincent and Hilliard are already yearning for the comforts of home. At the start of the central act, Vincent enquires: 'Is this the life that we admir'd in others, with envy at their happiness?' (III. i. p. 393; *Crew*, III. i. 1–2). The aristocratic literary and romanticized valorization of the innocence and carelessness of a country person's life is directly challenged by experience, as it is in those centrally placed exchanges between Corin the Shepherd and Touchstone the court jester in Shakespeare's pastoral comedy.

The moral emptiness of dressing up as gypsies and beggars is exposed and explored throughout the play. In another significant act of intertextuality, Brome's theme and his character of the Patrico or beggar-priest look back to a 1621 Ben Jonson court masque, *The Gipsies Metamorphosed*, which saw the court indulging in practice of this kind; and yet Brome also suggests that there are ways in which this countryside community is superior to the corrupt world of courts and cities he interrogates elsewhere in his dramatic canon. Even Oliver, Amie's brother and, in the central scene, the attempted rapist of Rachel and Meriel, recognizes the disparities: 'And there is much wholesomer flesh under country dirt than city painting, and less danger in dirt and rags, than in ceruse and satin' (III. i. pp. 401–2; *Crew*, III. i. 253-5).

One of the most affecting moments on the stage is a fourth-act passage of description relating to a marriage of two elderly beggars offstage for which there are great communal revels and celebrations. In a direct invocation of the same 'world turned upside-down' tradition of carnival that we saw Brome exploiting for political and social purpose in *The Antipodes* (see Chapter 4), we are provided in the midst of *A Jovial Crew* with images of the bride with her 'half-half-eye' and the groom on his crutches cutting a merry caper on the dance floor. Marriage as an institution undergoes some crucial re-evaluation in this play, with Amie's direct challenge to the patriarchal inscriptions and prescriptions of arranged marriage, and her own radical countryside contracting with Springlove.

A Jovial Crew maps out its social differentiations via linguistic demarcations: the play is skilfully divided between verse and prose, with the prose, for the most part, spoken by the rural commonwealth of beggars. The value of the life of the labouring poor is itself emphasized in a moment of literary and poetic self-awareness when the beggar-poet Scribble (author of the later metatheatrical play-within-a-play) observes: 'There's as good poetry in blank verse, as meter' (IV. ii. p. 428; *Crew*, IV. ii. 156). By this he refers to the beggars' ability to produce unrhymed but stressed verse of a quality equal to that of the quantitative style of verse – based on strict metrical and syllabic prosody – that would be the result of an élite poet's classical training. That this voice of egalitarianism sounds a good century and a half before William Wordsworth's claims for the blank-verse form in the *Preface to the Lyrical Ballads* is both striking and informing.

Even in the midst of their obvious discomforts, Vincent and Hilliard are perceptive enough to register the greater sense of community that the world in common of the beggars fosters:

> With them there is no grievance or perplexity;
> No fear of war, or state disturbances.
> No alteration in a commonwealth,
> Or innovation, shakes a thought of theirs.
>
> (IV. ii. p. 426; *Crew*, IV. ii. 90–3)

Hilliard echoes Vincent's observations by recording:

> We have no fear of lessening our estates;
> Nor any grudge with us (without taxation)
> To lend or give, upon command, the whole
> Strength of our wealth for public benefit;
>
> (IV. ii. p. 426; *Crew*, IV. ii. 95–8)

The language here is worth pausing to look at in detail. Brome's play was, as I mentioned at the start of this chapter, one of the last plays (possibly the last) to be performed before the outbreak of the civil war between King and parliament. It was played at the Cockpit Theatre in Drury Lane in 1641. In the dedicatory letter to Lord Stanley which Brome attached to the printed version of the playtext, he claims, 'All the arguments I can use to induce you to take notice of this thing of nothing is that it had the luck to tumble last of all in the epidemical ruin of the scene and now limps hither with a wooden leg to beg an alms at your hand' (p. 344; *Crew*, ll. 25–9). I am endlessly intrigued by how, in this description, Brome likens his play to the limping bride-groom of the carnivalesque wedding. In a seeming show of deference and submission, I would argue that the subversive potential of theatre is being consciously staked out.

What this prefatory letter indicates without a doubt is that Brome's play is a product of a troubled cultural moment; and the vocabulary of Vincent's and Hilliard's observations within the play proper further emphasizes this. Vincent talks of a world of grievances and perplexity. 'Grievances' had a specific parliamentary meaning: the submission of grievances by Parliament to the King in the form of the Petition of Right had been a cause of the 1629 dissolution and the instigation of Personal Rule. In 1641, when *A Jovial Crew* was written and performed, the tensions produced by that decade or so of non-parliamentary rule – not least by the monarch's abuse of prerogative in the levying of extraordinary taxations which may accord a particular freightage to that word in the context of Hilliard's previously quoted speech – were producing grim prophecies of their own. A direct comparison might be drawn between these and Oldrents's fear for his estates and his inheritance, since he is a member of the very section of the community that felt threatened. There was indeed 'alteration in the commonwealth' and a coming time of 'innovation' or revolution, that no-one could predict the course of, but of which many feared the consequences.

The pastoral genre was, I have suggested, embedded with implications of the court, and indeed the courtly, in the Caroline period and specifically throughout the 1630s. The form's employment and deployment on the public stages of theatres such as the Cockpit or the Blackfriars may, then, have been a strategic gesture, a gesture of opposition or of reappropriation by the public dramatists against or in critique of the court. I would argue that something similar can be read into reworkings of the masque genre in this non-courtly context.

The very precise pressures placed on local or regional communities by non-parliamentary government was, I suggested, a prime concern of Ben Jonson's own intervention into pastoral in *A Tale of a Tub*. That same world of local officialdom and authority is feared in Brome's play by the beggars' crew: 'the jaws of the justice, the clutch of the constable, the hooks of the headborough, and the biting blows of the beadle' (IV. ii. p. 425; *Crew*, IV. ii. 59–61), as they are alliteratively expressed, are embodied on the stage by the negative figure of Justice Clack, who sentences before he cross-examines and who presumes all are guilty until proven innocent. Corrupt Justices of the Peace are an interesting recurrence in plays from this period. From Justice Greedy (whose name says it all) in Massinger's *A New Way to Pay Old Debts* through Jonson's Justice Preamble in *A Tale of a Tub* to Brome's arbitrary patriarch Clack, they seem to expose the new potential for corruption under Charles I's exploitative and singular rule.

It is also no coincidence that a number of dramatists started to interrogate the possibilities and the ostensible parameters of pastoral in the 1630s: Jonson again looked to pastoral in 1637 in his unfinished last play, *The Sad Shepherd*. The usual critical response to that play has been to see it as a nostalgic piece of sub-Spenserian and sub-Shakespearean romance, with its mourning lover-knight Aeglamour, its cloned and assailed heroines, and its Robin Hood–Maid Marion folkloric framework. At the heart of the play, however, is a trenchant investigation of rural community as against the hierarchical quasi-aristocratic structures of dominant society. The operations of just such an (implicitly patriarchal) community upon individuals such as Maudlin the witch form the basis of the Sherwood-forest-based drama. The punishment and demonization of particular groups or individuals is captured astutely in George-a-Greene's observation that:

> I thought a Witch's banks
> Had enclosed nothing but the merry pranks
> Of some old woman.
>
> (Jonson, VII, II. viii. 36–8).

Pastoral, then, is employed on the Caroline public stage as a means of exploring notions of community and, in that, it has directly social and political implications. The opening moments of James Shirley's 1642 country-based play *The Sisters* makes this use of the politicized subject-matter of country communities overt. It should be emphasized that the country was the traditional seat of the gentry, that focus for opposition to the court and the crown that we were exploring in a town context in Chapter 4. The play begins in a forest in the company of a troupe of bandits, governed by the arch-pretender Frapolo, who is rejecting the edicts and proclamations of their ruler the Prince Farnese of Parma:

> We are safe within our woods and territories
> And are above his edicts. Have not we
> A commonwealth among ourselves, ye Tripolites?
> A commonwealth? a kingdom! and I am

The prince of Qui-va-las, your sovereign thief,
And you are all my subjects!

(Shirley, VI, I. i. p. 359)

Such declarations surely had resonance in 1642, when, as Shirley's Prologue tells us, the Caroline court had itself decamped from London to York. Power-centres were shifting and confused; and the fact that, later in the play, Frapolo will disguise himself as Prince Farnese in order to gain access to the mock-court of the vain Paulina (one of the two 'sisters' of the title, but who herself turns out to be a counterfeit noble by the end), only adds to the very disrupted and disturbed account of power and rule this play offers. Its real focus of dramatic and communal energy is undoubtedly the troupe of bandits who take on a series of masks and disguises in the course of the action. It is they, too, who offer a kind of morality amidst the moral confusions in the society of the play.

In *A Jovial Crew* Richard Brome, along with Shirley, Jonson, and others, is invoking and redetermining the pastoral genre to directly political ends. These very precise nuanced inflections of the vocabulary and discourse of the countryside and the 'Country' community were to prove significant in the civil wars and in the particular sympathies expressed by the regions in the conflict; social historians of the period have viewed them as crucial to a full understanding of the war and its progress. Genre is, then, a reflection and, indeed, inflection of contemporary concerns. Brome's prologue makes that distinction explicit in its expressed concern that 'in these sad and tragic days' comedy is no longer the favoured generic form. It may be that he is suggesting that tragedy is the dominant mode; but that phrase 'sad and tragic days' must have had a very particular resonance in 1641, with the threat of war looming on the horizon, a war that would be waged not against some external force, but that would pit brother against brother and household against household in a grim rewriting of the battles waged over love and land in Brome's and Shirley's vagabond plays.

Brome's Prologue stresses the romance element of *A Jovial Crew* (so linking it to the strictures and structures of Jonson's and Shirley's pastoral forerunners), and emphasizes how his lover-protagonists are in the course of the action 'Expos'd to strange adventures through the briers | Of love and fate' (p. 351;

67

Crew, ll. 18–19). Undoubtedly in this period Romance and Pastoral were, as genres, associated with the self-representations of the Caroline Personal Rule. To rewrite and revise them thus on the public stage could be seen as a deliberately subversive social gesture by Brome, Shirley, Jonson, and others. Martin Butler has argued as much in his book *Theatre and Crisis*.

Theatre itself has a pregnant and potentially subversive role to play in the plotline of *A Jovial Crew*. The fifth and final act is essentially given over to the performance of the beggars' play. A bill of fare is offered to the onstage audience: Oldrents (by this stage a guest in Justice Clack's household, and one who is given the play performance as an act of appeasement after he complains of the Justice's poor hospitality) is offered such plays as *The Two Lost Daughters*, *The Vagrant Steward*, *The Old Squire and the Fortune-Teller*, and *The Beggar's Prophecy*. Oldrents rejects all these as touching too much on his own life and therefore likely to send him back into the fit of melancholy we saw him writhing under at the start of *A Jovial Crew*. Brome toys here with the close relationship between theatre's carnivalesque game-playings and the real world just beyond its frame.

Justice Clack provides a similarly anxious audience, constantly fretting about how justice will be performed and represented. The irony, of course, is the implicit criticism Brome's character-ization of Clack offers to the real watching audience in the Cockpit. Sentwell's offer of comfort is equally rich in ironic implication, not least for Charles I: 'Pray sir, be not severe; they act kings and emperors as well as justices. And justice is blind they say: you may therefore be pleased to wink a little' (V. i. p. 437; *Crew*, V. i. 111–3). The play is as a whole deeply critical of overly restrictive and demanding patriarchs, a fact figured variously in Oldrents's overly managerial approach to the lives of his two daughters and his steward (later his son), and in Clack's oppressive sentencing. In a manner akin to plays such as *The Weeding of Covent Garden*, the space of the family is used as a means for exploring the wider problems of the monarch-father's relationship with his children-subjects in the body politic or wider commonwealth. Theatre and truth are intimately con-nected, it seems: theatre relies on the contemporary situation for its material and fabric, however transformed in practice that material might appear.

The play performed by the beggars (in connecting actors and vagabonds thus Brome is playing on a popular stereotype of travelling players) is:

> no dainty wit of court
> Nor city pageantry, nor country sport:
> But a plain piece of action, short and sweet;
> In story true.

(V. i. p. 443; Crew, V. i. 304–7)

The beggars' play is the story of a Utopia or a commonwealth, a title which directly imitates that of Sir Thomas More's Tudor textual ruminations on an 'ideal' society. That text, that 'fiction', has also been recognized as having topical political and social resonances and concerns. By the time of Brome's play a word like 'commonwealth' contained the possible meaning of 'republic' – of a non-absolutist state or nation – in an even more pressing sense than in More's life. Within a decade of the first performance of Brome's drama the king would have been executed in the 1640s' most dramatic public performance, and the English common-wealth inaugurated. In recognition of this fact, when the Royal Shakespeare Company revived the play for performance in 1992 it commissioned the contemporary dramatist Stephen Jeffreys to adapt the extant script. Perhaps the most significant alteration Jeffreys made was to make far more explicit what he saw as the republican undertow to the themes and events of the play. His ending saw Rachel but not Meriel re-absorbed into the patriarchal heart of Oldrents's home, and Meriel rejoining the beggar's republic for a life of egalitarianism and political democracy. That might be too radical a reading of Brome's text as it stands, but it is worth noting that his own play within a play is about the spatial and theoretical conflicts between country, city, and court which I have been suggesting throughout this book were central to the representations and concerns of Caroline drama at this time and in particular during the period of Personal Rule (1629–40). The Beggar-Poet says of his drama: 'I would have the country, the city and the court be at great variance for superiority. Then would I have Divinity and Law stretch their wide throats to appease and reconcile them' (IV. ii. p. 430; Crew, IV. ii. 207–10). In a chilling prefiguring of the ensuing wartime years of bloody battles, the soldier steps in to cudgel all parts of

69

society into submission; but only the beggar – the true spirit of community, as we have seen in the play proper – can truly reconcile and resolve all. This was Brome's social Utopian vision: the fissures and fractures of the world of the play proper and the world of 1641 which it so persistently acknowledges suggested that reality might prove rather different.

Oldrents's name derives from the fact that he offers his tenants a reasonable rent on their estate houses and land in comparison to the exploitations of his contemporary land-owners in the seventeenth century. Between 1600 and 1688 rents increased threefold in England. There is, then, a case for seeing Brome's play as another act of political and social nostalgia for a better time – a reading that would align him with the dominant strain of critical interpretations of Massinger and *A New Way to Pay Old Debts* and Jonson and *A Tale of a Tub*. I want to suggest, however, that Oldrents is no different to the patriarchs criticized and critiqued elsewhere in the canon of Caroline drama, not least by Brome himself, in plays such as *The English Moor, or the Mock-Marriage* (another attack on the institution of arranged marriage), *The Weeding of Covent Garden*, and *The Antipodes*. Oldrents's own estate is founded on historical oppression – the eviction and displacement of the Patrico's grandfather, Wrought-on – and his family proves as imperfect as many others with the revelation of the existence of his bastard child. Primogeniture from this angle looks a distinctly shaky institution on which to found the inheritance, maintenance, and management of land. The old institutions, as in Massinger's *A New Way to Pay Old Debts*, are crumbling, and what the ruminations on the countryside in these Caroline pastorals look to is the formation of a new society, a new sense of community: a new way to pay old debts indeed.

The historian Christopher Hill has argued that the upheavals of the seventeenth century are essentially a battle over land rights and territory (Hill). This is not to downplay the role of religious and social conflict in the period, but it is to realize a basic truth about the Caroline plays we have been considering here: that it is the spatial dimensions of these plays and their sites of performance that may give us the greatest clue to the tensions and the manifestations of the period they contain; and that, as ever, it is in the dynamics and the space of performance that the essential aspects of the society that both produced them and which were in part produced by them might be revealed. Oldrents may claim in *A Jovial Crew* that 'True stories and true jests do seldom thrive on stages' (V. i. p. 444; *Crew*, V. i. 308), but I think that Richard Brome here has the last laugh on the reigning monarch of his play community and that, in the assertion of the truth of the opposite point, that theatre is often a direct inflection of its moment of creation, the public theatre offered a genuine warning to Charles I that the real monarch might have done well to heed. By 1642 the public-theatre flags had been taken down and ensigns of a very different kind raised in the fields and spaces of a far less esoteric contest of wits. It has been my argument here that Philip Massinger, John Ford, James Shirley, and Richard Brome, amongst others, were chroniclers of the events and debates leading up to that moment, and that their plays offer us a striking account of one of the most exciting moments of British political, social, and theatrical history.

Select Bibliography

GENERAL CRITICISM AND HISTORY

Bulman, James, 'Caroline Drama', in A. R. Braunmuller and Michael Hattaway (eds), *The Cambridge Companion to English Renaissance Drama* (Cambridge: Cambridge University Press, 1990), 353–79.

Butler, Martin, *Theatre and Crisis, 1632–42* (Cambridge: Cambridge University Press, 1984).

Clark, Ira, *Professional Playwrights: Massinger, Ford, Shirley, and Brome* (Lexington: University of Kentucky Press, 1992).

Gurr, Andrew, *The Shakespearean Stage 1574–1642*, 2nd edn (Cambridge: Cambridge University Press, 1980).

Hill, Christopher, *Puritanism and Revolution* (London: Mercury, 1962).

Sharpe, Kevin, *The Personal Rule of Charles I* (New Haven: Yale University Press, 1992).

Tomlinson, Sophie, '"She That Plays the King": Henrietta Maria and the Threat of the Actress in Caroline Culture', in Gordon McMullan and Jonathan Hope (eds), *The Politics of Tragicomedy* (London: Routledge, 1992), 189–207.

Tricomi, Albert, *Anticourt Drama, 1603–1642* (Charlottesville: University of Virginia Press, 1989).

Veevers, Erica, *Images of Love and Religion: Queen Henrietta Maria and Court Entertainments* (Cambridge: Cambridge University Press, 1989).

PHILIP MASSINGER

Editions

The Plays and Poems of Philip Massinger, ed. Philip Edwards and Colin Gibson, 5 vols (Oxford: Clarendon Press, 1976).

Selected Plays of Philip Massinger, ed. Colin Gibson (Cambridge: Cambridge University Press, 1978). Contains *The Duke of Milan*, *The Roman Actor*, *A New Way to Pay Old Debts*, and *The City Madam*.

A New Way to Pay Old Debts, ed. T. W. Craik (London: Ernest Benn, 1964).
A New Way to Pay Old Debts is also included in *Four Jacobean City Comedies*, ed. Gamini Salgado (Harmondsworth: Penguin, 1975).
The City Madam, ed. T. W. Craik (London: Ernest Benn, 1964).
The City Madam, ed. Cyrus Hoy (London: Arnold, 1964).

Criticism

Braunmuller, A. R. and J. C. Bulman (eds), *Comedy from Shakespeare to Sheridan* (Newark: University of Delaware Press, 1986). Several essays dealing with Massinger.

Butler, Martin, 'Massinger's *The City Madam* and the Caroline Audience', *Renaissance Drama*, n.s., 13 (1982), 157–87.

—— 'Massinger's Grim Comedy', in Michael Cordner, Peter Holland, and John Kerrigan (eds), *English Comedy* (Cambridge: Cambridge University Press, 1994), 119–36.

—— 'The Outsider as Insider', in David L. Smith, Richard Strier, and David Bevington (eds), *The Theatrical City: Culture, Theatre and Politics in London 1576–1649* (Cambridge: Cambridge University Press, 1995), 193–208.

Clark, Ira, *The Moral Art of Philip Massinger* (Lewisburg: Bucknell University Press, 1992).

Howard, Douglas (ed.), *Philip Massinger: A Critical Reassessment* (Cambridge: Cambridge University Press, 1985).

Lindley, Keith, 'Noble Scarlet *vs.* London Blue', in David L. Smith, Richard Strier, and David Bevington (eds), *The Theatrical City: Culture, Theatre and Politics in London 1576–1649* (Cambridge: Cambridge University Press, 1995), 183–92.

JOHN FORD

Editions

The Works of John Ford, ed. W. Gifford and A. J. Dyce, 3 vols (London: J. Toovey, 1869).

'*Tis Pity She's a Whore and Other Plays*, ed. Marion Lomax (Oxford: Oxford University Press, 1995). Contains *The Lover's Melancholy*, *The Broken Heart*, '*Tis Pity She's a Whore*, and *Perkin Warbeck*.

Ford: Three Plays, ed. Keith Sturgess (Harmondsworth: Penguin, 1970). Contains '*Tis Pity She's a Whore*, *The Broken Heart*, and *Perkin Warbeck*.

Selected Plays of John Ford, ed. Colin Gibson (Cambridge: Cambridge University Press, 1986). Contains *The Broken Heart*, '*Tis Pity She's a Whore* and *Perkin Warbeck*.

The Broken Heart, ed. Brian Morris (London: Ernest Benn, 1965).

The Lover's Melancholy, ed. R. F. Hill (Manchester: Manchester University Press, 1985).

Perkin Warbeck, ed. Peter Ure (London: Methuen, 1968).

'Tis Pity She's a Whore, ed. N. W. Bawcutt (London: Arnold, 1966).

'Tis Pity She's a Whore, ed. Brian Morris (London: Ernest Benn, 1968).

'Tis Pity She's a Whore, ed. Derek Roper (London: Methuen, 1975).

The Witch of Edmonton, in *Three Jacobean Witchcraft Plays*, ed. Peter Corbin and Douglas Sedge (Manchester: Manchester University Press, 1986).

Criticism

Anderson, D. K. (ed.), *'Concord in Discord': The Plays of John Ford 1586–1986* (New York: AMS, 1986).

Barton, Anne, 'He That Plays the King: Ford's *Perkin Warbeck* and the Stuart History Play' in Marie Axton and Raymond Williams (eds), *English Drama: Forms and Development* (Cambridge: Cambridge University Press, 1977), 69–93.

Farr, Dorothy M., *John Ford and the Caroline Theatre* (London: Macmillan, 1979).

Hopkins, Lisa, *John Ford's Political Theatre* (Manchester: Manchester University Press, 1994).

Neill, Michael (ed.), *John Ford: Critical Re-Visions* (Cambridge: Cambridge University Press, 1988).

Wiseman, Susan J., ' *'Tis Pity She's a Whore*: Representing the Incestuous Body', in Lucy Gent and Nigel Llewellyn (eds), *Renaissance Bodies: The Human Figure in English Culture c.1540–1660* (London: Reaktion, 1990), 180–97.

Wymer, Rowland, *Webster and Ford* (London: Macmillan, 1995).

JAMES SHIRLEY

Editions

Dramatic Works, ed. W. Gifford and A. J. Dyce, 6 vols (London: J. Murray, 1833).

The Cardinal, ed. E. M. Yearling (Manchester: Manchester University Press, 1986).

Hyde Park, ed. Simon Trussler (London: Methuen; RSC Programme/Text, 1987).

The Lady of Pleasure, ed. Ronald Huebert (Manchester: Manchester University Press, 1986).

The Traitor, ed. John Stewart Carter (London: Arnold, 1965).

Criticism

Burner, Sandra A., *James Shirley: A Study of Literary Coteries and Patronage in Seventeenth-Century England* (London and New York: University Press of America, 1989).

Gaby, Rosemary, 'Of Vagabonds and Commonwealths: *Beggars' Bush, A Jovial Crew*, and *The Sisters*', *Studies in English Literature*, 34 (1994), 401–24.

Lucow, Ben, *James Shirley* (Boston: Twayne, 1981).

Traub, Valerie, 'The (In)significance of 'Lesbian' Desire in Early Modern England' in Susan Zimmerman (ed.), *Erotic Politics: Desire on the Renaissance Stage* (London: Routledge, 1992), 150–69.

Walker, Kim, '"New Prison": Representing the Female Actor in Shirley's *The Bird in a Cage*', *English Literary Renaissance*, 21 (1991), 383–400.

Wertheim, Albert, 'Games and Courtship in James Shirley's *Hyde Park*', *Anglia*, 90 (1972), 71–91.

RICHARD BROME

Editions

Dramatic Works, ed. John Pearson, 3 vols (London: Pearson, 1873).

The Antipodes, ed. Ann Haaker (London: Arnold, 1968).

An edition of *The Antipodes* can also be found in *Three Renaissance Travel Plays*, ed. Anthony Parr (Manchester: Manchester University Press, 1995).

The English Moor, or The Mock-Marriage, ed. Sara Jayne Steen (Columbia: University of Missouri Press, 1983).

A Jovial Crew, ed. Ann Haaker (London: Arnold, 1966).

Jeffreys, Stephen and Richard Brome, *A Jovial Crew* (London: Warner Chappell, 1992). The Royal Shakespeare Company adaptation of 1992.

Criticism

Donaldson, Ian, *The World Upside Down: Comedy from Jonson to Fielding* (Oxford: Oxford University Press, 1970). Useful on *The Antipodes*.

Gaby, Rosemary, 'Of Vagabonds and Commonwealths: *Beggars' Bush, A Jovial Crew*, and *The Sisters*', *Studies in English Literature*, 34 (1994), 401–24.

Sanders, Julie, 'The Politics of Escapism: Fantasies of Travel and Power in Richard Brome's *The Antipodes* and Ben Jonson's *The Alchemist*', in Ceri Sullivan and Barbara White (eds), *Writing and Fantasy* (London: Longman, 1998), 137–50.

Shaw, Catherine, *Richard Brome* (Boston: Twayne, 1980).

Index

Printed and bound by CPI Group (UK) Ltd, Croydon, CR0 4YY

13/04/2025